3—

MEANING IN CRAFTS

Haniwa decorated horse, Japanese, fifth century. Haniwa figures and animals were set up in circles around the base of burial mounds to hold back the earth. Most were constructed hastily of clay cylinders made by skilled but primitive craftsmen. They were made hollow so that they would dry faster. Some experts believe these haniwa ("clay circle") figures substituted for live people and animals that at one time were buried with their dead masters. This terra cotta horse is almost three feet high. Courtesy of The Art Institute of Chicago.

MEANING IN CRAFTS

EDWARD L. MATTIL

Chairman, Department of Art
North Texas State University

THIRD EDITION

Prentice-Hall, Inc., Englewood Cliffs, New Jersey

Illustration on p. i courtesy of The Art Institute of Chicago.

© 1971 by Prentice-Hall, Inc., Englewood Cliffs, N.J.

13–567156–6

Library of Congress Catalog Card Number: 73–123087

Printed in the United States of America

Current printing (last number):

10 9 8 7 6 5 4 3 2

PRENTICE-HALL INTERNATIONAL, INC., London
PRENTICE-HALL OF AUSTRALIA, PTY. LTD., Sydney
PRENTICE-HALL OF CANADA, LTD., Toronto
PRENTICE-HALL OF INDIA PRIVATE LIMITED, New Delhi
PRENTICE-HALL OF JAPAN, INC., Tokyo

FOREWORD

Like the earlier editions, this book was prepared to assist those who work with young people, especially those whose ambition is to teach more effectively. The increasing depersonalization in our culture makes it important to direct more attention to those activities that strengthen our self concepts, and to maintain and fully develop those qualities that make for creativity. This is not a simple task, for every new automated or computerized process seems to cause a greater detachment from the more fundamental things in life, and research has shown a steady decline, even a permanent loss, of creativity where there are no supporting programs or where programs suppress creativity.

This book is offered to the classroom teacher so that he may more fully understand the philosophical basis for crafts in education, and learn better methods of teaching crafts to children. It offers, too, some understanding of the significance of crafts in this and other cultures. It makes no attempt to provide all the answers, for it is the teacher who must develop a sound teaching philosophy and who must use his own imagination, ingenuity, and intuition to develop an effective program.

The processes and materials serve only as the means of providing some of the essential conditions in which creativeness can flourish and in which children can begin to fulfill their potential. Most important is the climate that the teacher establishes—it can be either one in which children can easily learn or one in which learning is stultified; it can be one in which imagination, invention, and inquiry accompany learning or one in which learning is crippled by the fear of error or by inflexible, unsupporting conditions.

When we understand how greatly learning is accelerated when children are encouraged to be perceptive, aware, and sensitive, then we understand the significance of art education. Experience in art sharpens all the senses, and thus helps to increase each child's capability.

This book is dedicated to those who accept the enormous responsibility of determining our future by being the teachers of today's young people. Teaching is one of the great adventures of the human spirit in which one neither gives nor receives, but instead shares with his fellow man.

My special gratitude goes to Marilyn Shobaken for the excellent design of this publication. My fondest recognition goes to Polly and Michael, the two people most interested in and supportive of everything I attempt.

ELM

CONTENTS

CONTENTS

three

PRINTING AND PRINTMAKING

six

SEASONAL ACTIVITIES AND THE
HOLIDAYS

seven

CERAMICS

eight
PAPIER-MÂCHE AND MASK-MAKING   171

nine
FABRICS   193

ten
POTPOURRI   211

bibliography

1-1

one

MEANING IN CRAFTS

Our language is full of words having multiple meanings. This creates many problems in understanding. Two such words are *art* and *craft*. When we think of each of these words without special context we may be thinking of a particular object or group of objects or, we may be thinking of a process. If we think of these words in relation to children they take on still another meaning for us. For our purposes, this book will be primarily concerned with various types of creative activity for children and youth in which an original product is the result of the experiences. These art and craft activities should be part of each child's art education. The illustrations and some of the text focus in part on that universal thread that seems to run through all history in which man, as a craftsman, continually made new demands on his originality, knowledge, skills, sensibilities, and experience in order to invest the objects he made with some special value, either practical or aesthetic. It is this same series of demands which the child learns to apply to his own work in art and craft activities that make art education an essential part of each child's development.

Today's artist/craftsman has largely adopted a position which is compatible with today's art education. Dedicated to the idea of personal freedom and in the midst of great varieties of old and new materials, he has turned crafts into a great creative adventure of the human spirit. Not trapped by tradition and unafraid of the newer technology, he has chosen to be inventive, risk-taking, and free to make mistakes. All of this represents a departure from the past for, until this century few crafts were made with the intention of having them as works of art. Rather, most crafts were created for practical purposes in the household or in industry or, they were used in religious ritual, social activities, theatre, and entertainment. So, today's artist/craftsmen like today's children and youth are less concerned with the practical or functional purposes of crafts. They are interested

Figure 1-1. Most people are conditioned to look only in museums for works of art, often unaware that they are surrounded by the beautiful products of highly skilled craftsmen. This elegant doorway, constructed of forged bronze by Sidney Simon, reflects the sensitivity of a craftsman who has taken a functional problem and made it into a work of art. (Downstate Medical Center, Brooklyn, N.Y.)

1-2

1-3

Figure 1-2. Work is one thing, workmanship another. Crafts might be thought of as the link between art and science, for the craftsman couples artistic invention to scientific knowledge of the possibilities and limitations of tools and materials. The inability to use tools would prevent the most imaginative person from carrying out his ideas. The craftsman enjoys and respects his tools. This jack-plane of Adolphus Frederick of Sweden, made about 1748, has been beautifully carved and decorated by its maker. Similar decorations are found on the handles of axes, hammers, and knives. (Nordiska Museet Arkiv)

Figure 1-3. This fantasy "Rooster Desk" by Thomas Simpson is constructed of wood and painted with acrylic polymer. It reflects the increasing lack of concern of the contemporary craftsmen for the "form follows function" theory of design. The craftsman is more concerned with the expression of his idea, the nature of his materials, and the extent to which he gives the object a quality that transcends function, material, or processes—he seeks to create a form of art. (Museum of Contemporary Crafts of the American Craftsmen's Council)

in instilling their crafts objects with originality, imagination, expression and meaning—those qualities essential to a work of art.

When we attempt to trace the historical development of crafts, we become engaged in the examination of almost any piece of hand workmanship that might have a claim to beauty, or, for that matter, any piece to which decoration has been applied. If in such a study we should be privileged to visit a native potter in rural India working at his primitive wheel, we might ask him, "Why did you become an artist?" To this he might reply, "I am not an artist. I am a potter, as were my father and grandfather; in fact, my family have always been potters. We are even *called* 'Potter.'" Curiously we may ask, "But isn't pottery art?" To this the potter may return, "No, it is a livelihood, my industry." Yet by our concepts of art and crafts, this potter may well be an artist as well as a craftsman engaging in his little industry, for as Herbert Read says, "The man who makes becomes potentially, or partially, an artist the moment the things he makes express or excite feeling." In a study of the history of crafts it soon becomes clear that artistic activity is not limited to a particular group of privileged people, rather it is a characteristic of most humans regardless of their education or their level of sophistication.

We must assume that the earliest tools and utensils of man were restricted to the considerations of utility. As their efficiency improved, there was a steady evolution of form. In any situation where people were first required to produce the necessities of life by hand, the useful concern was of prime importance and as long as impoverished or stringent conditions continued, the art quality of the object rarely exceeded the functional design of the object. However, as soon as time and skill permitted, the craftsman was fairly sure to elaborate or decorate his objects and it was at this point in man's development where the matter of choice entered into the picture. For example, when man became able to create a variety of clay bowls, each good for holding grain or water, he found himself engaged in the process of making judgments—practical and *aesthetic*—in determining form and decoration.

These are the same problems which are part of crafts teaching in the elementary school. In crafts and art education, we are able to teach procedures—and every child can learn procedures. However, it is while the procedures are being carried out that the child engages in constant choices or judgments. He may decide why one shape is "better" than another, or he may intuitively select or eliminate in order to arrive at the "best" choice. This selection or choice, in which he constantly engages, is aesthetic judgment, which, it can be assumed, cannot be developed without activities that call upon the constant use of these qualities, which are basically the ones that distinguish man.

It is at this very point that there are many disagreements regarding the teaching of arts and crafts, for many teachers are unable to distinguish between procedures and technique. Procedures are the various activities that can be explained within the general framework of the project being introduced. Technique, on the other hand, is the highly individualized use of the materials involved; it is the child's personal "language" or "handwriting" with materials. It is impossible to teach technique, for it simply must grow out of the child's need to express himself. The teacher who believes that technique is something that can be taught may well be only imposing his own technique upon the child. Impositions will ultimately become handicaps. It is safe, then, to say that one can teach procedures and may help the child only to develop his own technique and that aesthetic judgment can develop only when the child has the freedom to make choices in his work.

Our schools cannot limit the teaching of crafts to only a few processes of the artist/craftsman. The constant development of new materials in every industry suggests an ever-widening area in crafts. Surely clay, wood, weaving, needlework, and many others of the "old standards" will maintain their importance, but it is necessary not to become so bound by traditional materials that one excludes the many exciting possibilities of experimentation with new materials and new processes. It is, however, very easy to become lost in the jungle of gimmicks and gadgets and to conduct a crafts program without depth or meaning. This usually becomes what is commonly called the "product-centered program." When such a program is in effect, the child rarely has the time or sufficient skill with tools or materials to carry out fully his imaginative ideas. Instead he seeks shortcuts in craftsmanship and hides behind a shield of indifference.

A truly creative student is not indifferent to what he does. Rather he dips deeply into his imagination, creates new and necessary symbols, develops personal techniques, and uses his tools with the maximum of skill. He discovers order in creative activity, finding pleasure in form, a personal attachment for the object on which he works, and a respect for his tools and materials. It is important that the crafts program be balanced to provide opportunities for fast, short-time projects using a great many materials in a large variety of ways as well as a number of basic arts and crafts experiences that are pursued in depth. This means that throughout the school life of the child, some activities, such as modeling, drawing, and printmaking are a regular part of the art program at every level. By repeatedly using the tools and materials of a few processes, the child can gain the skill necessary for him to carry out his ideas directly without always having to learn to use the tools first. When the child's attention is focused primarily on the use of a new tool and the discoveries that accompany it, he is generally unable to focus fully on what he wishes to say with the tools. Ideally, the tool or material should become the extension of the child's thinking, not the focus for it.

Although there is a case for depth approaches to crafts teaching, the schools

Figure 1-4. The creative urge is universal, but it must be developed. So often this development is ignored or left to chance so that there is a steady decline in the creative ability of children during their school years. Art education is one of the areas in which a high premium is placed on creative thinking and expression at all levels of development. But education in general must establish the fostering of creative expression as one of its prime goals.

Figure 1-5. It is important to plan experiences of good quality and to interrelate them, so that learning can be cumulative. The creative teacher does not become paralyzed by a rigid system of lessons, but uses every good spontaneous experience as a basis for creative expression by the children. The strongest motivations are intense personal experiences. (Photograph by Ed Leos)

1-6   1-7

Figure 1-6. Dolls appear in many cultures and in all periods of history. Their use is almost always the same, as playthings for children. Their styles differ greatly because of the interpretations of various cultures, the skill in craftsmanship, and the kinds of materials available for use. This German stick doll of the nineteenth century is carved of wood, a material very familiar to the German craftsman. Its movable arms and legs are jointed with leather. Smoothly sanded and heavily painted, the doll has a finished, almost sophisticated look. (The Smithsonian Institution)

Figure 1-7. This humorous figure by artist Carol Anthony is a combination of papier-mâché, linen, enamel paint, and assorted odds and ends. It exemplifies the freedom of the American craftsman to experiment, to be unafraid of mistakes, to take risks—in essence, not to be bogged down in tradition. Rather, today's craftsman turns crafts into a creative adventure. (Museum of Contemporary Crafts of the American Craftsmen's Council)

would err if crafts were limited to just a few processes. The school is one of the main instruments for the development of children's potentiality, and it is up to the school to provide the conditions that foster such development. One of the main conditions is opportunity, where materials and facilities are present to try out one's potential. Such a program allows for the opportunity to try one's ability in a variety of activities and to repeat with regularity those activities of special interest to the individual. Another condition is the presence of a mature and sensitive adult, who guides, suggests, evaluates, and encourages the child. Such a teacher grows as the child grows, enjoys as the child enjoys, and *cares*. The teacher creates the environment, whether it be rich or impoverished. It is the teacher who surrounds the child with experiences that keep him feeding on the stuff of learning, growing, and living. People, like turtles or snails, will come out of their shells for something enhancing and will stay inside when threatened. The threatening environment is frequently built upon prevention—prevention of waste, prevention of movement, prevention of soiled clothes, prevention of accidents. How terribly uninspiring it is to have a lesson begin with "Now don't make any mistakes; don't soil your tables; don't spill the paint; don't cut your fingers; don't, don't, don't." Equally important as a factor that represses creative work are restrictions on curiosity and manipulativeness. Children are curious by nature. They come to us all perception—ready to smell, touch, taste, feel, look, think, and ask about everything. As R. Buckminster Fuller says[1], "I think that all humans are born artist-scientist-inventors but life progressively squelches the individual's drives and capabilities. As a consequence, by the time most humans mature they have lost one, two or all three of those fundamental self starters."

Given a chance to develop sensitively, without undue restrictions, the child learns quickly. He not only absorbs everything from his environment, but he also soon restructures what he takes in—in his own symbols, combining it with his imagination and his fantasy. It is unwise for the parent or teacher to try to eliminate fantasy from the child's thinking. The child, in his moments of creative freedom, does not set out consciously to create a new art object. Rather, he gives the object of his attention and effort the value and the power of humanness.

In the same way that our schools cannot limit the teaching of crafts to a few processes, they cannot limit it to a few children. Children may be likened to a handful of seeds from many flowers. At first they may seem similar in many respects. Place these seeds in the earth and nourish them. As they grow and mature, their differences become marked. Some remain small and delicate, while others are large and brilliant; some bloom early and some late. One thing they have in common: under good conditions, they all bloom and have their own beauty.

---

[1] *The Arts and Man,* Chapter V, Prentice-Hall, Inc. 1969.

Our classrooms are the earth for these seeds, and when fertile and rich, they bring forth the best. But the classroom can also have the stultifying effect of poor soil in which nothing can grow. This good soil-poor soil analogy can also be applied to the kind of motivations that are used to introduce various crafts. The child may be given the best kind of instruction in procedures and may use the best materials, but if he has nothing to express through the process, it becomes a meaningless, mechanical experience. In crafts, the child is able to organize his thoughts, ideas, feelings, actions, and technique into a product. He takes paints, fibers, clay, wood, stone, and metals and reorganizes and reforms them in to a product which is an interpretation of his experience. If the experience or motivation is shallow, the ideas vague, the feelings diffuse or absent, the product will reflect it. In other words, the product is the record of the complete process. The creative arts and crafts of children have the power of reordering thoughts and experience in their image.

With the very young child, the process exceeds the product in importance. For example, the five- or six-year-old child may, day after day, pound out balls or coils of clay, finally joining them into very simple figure concepts. This daily repetition is of prime importance, for it is only through this repetition that the child gains the sureness of achievement that is necessary for growth of confidence. One must then paint to learn to paint, or pound to learn to pound, or assemble to learn to assemble. In these early efforts, which are significant to growth, the teacher is unwise to place undue emphasis upon the products as such. Rather should the emphasis be placed upon continued good experiences with materials and a continued involvement in the process. In these earliest efforts the child is developing a valid system of communication.

The problem of process as it relates to product is a constant topic for discussion. Yet it is a reasonably easy concept to grasp. Both the process and the product are of importance in creative craft activities. However, in the earliest years, when the child's ideas come rapidly and do not remain for long, when interest spans are short and motor skill limited, the emphasis is more upon the process of creating. During this early phase the product is important as a record of the child's involvement, growth, and level of development. We may be sure that occasionally we shall find a veritable gem of child art that we wish to preserve. However, we err when we start with the intention of firing all the ceramic work of a kindergarten class, for here we focus more upon the product than upon the child and his experience in creating a product. The mere fact that the product is made of a permanent or semipermanent material may cause the teacher, consciously or subconsciously, to impose adult concepts and standards on the children's work. This does not mean that the teacher is without standards. Indeed, we all have standards, some high and some unfortunately not so high. But the standards that are applied must relate to the standards that each child must form for himself.

This requires that the teacher be critical without being damaging, be selective without being biased, be able to direct without being dogmatic, be inspiring without establishing the ultimate goal, be patient without being indifferent, praise sincerely and freely without being indiscriminate. The truly creative teacher is never sure he is right, never bound by lock-step methods. He has the feeling he is on the right path, but when he is absolutely sure that he is right about all of his teaching, he is in danger of becoming dull and dogmatic. H. L. Mencken once said, "It is the dull man who is sure and the sure man who is dull."

As the child grows older, it is only natural that the product continually gains in importance, until as adults it is no longer possible to do creative work if there are no products to give personal satisfaction. Adults simply cannot be satisfied only by the process.

In early childhood, when imagination is unfettered, crafts serve as a wholesome outlet for the many fantasies that come into the young mind. Every new thing ever created resulted from the imaginative ability of someone who could imagine or dream beyond the realities of his known world. Children need to have the time to wonder, ponder, and dream, and to have a positive outlet for their imaginations. It is just as important that the child develop his powers of imagination as it is for him to develop in social or group activities. It is important for teachers to foster in children the attitude of expecting and liking to work out their own problems, instead of yielding to others who may try to force them into accepting ready-made solutions. At the same time, they must be shown the need for being able to work with others toward common goals, and not to be so self-centered as to be unable to accept criticism and to weigh the ideas of others.

All of us want to see children grow to express themselves clearly—and to have something worth expressing. If we recall the number of misses Johnny made before he learned to coordinate sufficiently to catch a thrown ball, we will have some idea of the struggle each child has to develop a personal concept in arts or crafts. It is only through this struggle with himself that the child truly grows. Think of the child whose parents never let him struggle, but who make every decision for him. When finally on his own and forced to make a decision, he is unable to do so. Crafts teaching, then, becomes not only the teaching of procedures, but also the creating of problems that call for personal solutions. A work of art is the report of discoveries the artist has made about his environment—and himself. How often we have seen the teacher who has the ready-made solution for art or crafts in the form of hectograph patterns? He carefully directs the group through every step, selecting and deciding for them, only to arrive with thirty identical products that are as unchildlike as they are uncreative. Such activities not only destroy the opportunity for growth through art experiences, but may even affect the child's confidence in his own ability to create.

1-8

1-9

What, then, are the basic considerations for the classroom teacher who wishes to use craft activities as an important part of the educational program of children?

CRAFT ACTIVITIES ARE CREATIVE ACTIVITIES

All children possess a creative instinct. Sound education provides the climate for the fullest development of this instinct. In crafts, each project must allow the child to think originally and to learn to work independently. Creative children work freely and flexibly; that is, they attack each problem without the fear of failure. Such freedom must be carefully preserved. The work of highly creative children is not always easy for the teacher, accustomed only to traditional approaches, to understand and value. A prerequisite for truly creative outcomes is the willingness of the child and the teacher to divorce themselves from the obvious and to work toward fresh approaches. This eliminates the cliché, the stereotype, and the banal.

It is an endless source of amazement to observe how creative children can quickly become detached from what exists conventionally and begin working energetically to construct something of their own to replace it. The teacher who begins his teaching with dogma, rules, techniques, or patterns will certainly be placing stumbling blocks that can easily destroy both the urge and the ability to create. The preservation and fostering of creative thinking and working in children should be the most important goal of education—not just of art education.

OPPORTUNITIES FOR GROWTH THROUGH CRAFTS

Education has always considered intellectual development as one of its main objectives. More recently we have come to consider other areas of growth as equally important. Children need to grow creatively, socially, physically, emotionally, and aesthetically. Each of these areas of growth should be evidenced in a crafts program that is truly planned to meet the needs of children.

Creative growth may be seen in the originality of ideas, while social growth

---

Figure 1-8. In a few remote villages of Switzerland the people still hold carnivals on special occasions. They wear masks like these; or they may dress in sheepskins and wear very gruesome masks to present a frightening appearance. When they wear the pleasant masks they are usually friendly to the crowd and distribute sweets. Swiss masks are either ugly and evil-looking or beautiful and pleasant, depending upon the occasion. (Schweizerisches Museum for Volkerkunde, Bazel)

Figure 1-9. Personal objects like this elaborate Spanish comb of carved chestnut wood were made during the Renaissance. They grew out of a theory that every object of human use, even the unimportant, could share in the beauty and harmony that were thought to be special qualities of the human mind. Many great artists of the time did not consider it beneath their dignity to provide designs for furniture, clothing, and small objects for domestic use. (Museo Arqueologico Nacional; Madrid)

may be seen in the child's increasing ability to work cooperatively in his group—in his increasing social responsibility and appreciation of the needs and feelings of others. Physical growth is easily identified through increasing motor control and the child's ability to coordinate mind, eye, and hand. Emotional growth is recognized in the child's ability to identify with his own work. This is the ability to express personal feelings or experiences without a dependency upon stereotypes or clichés. The aesthetic growth of the child appears with an increasing sensitivity to the organization of ideas and feeling by means of the materials, form, color, and texture. Where aesthetic growth is not present, the child is unable to integrate his thinking, feeling, and perceiving into a harmonious organization.

The more the classroom teacher is aware of these many facets of growth, the more able he is to provide a crafts program with meaning, in which crafts become a means of education and not an end in themselves. Art can touch all phases of human life, making it richer and more beautiful.

OPPORTUNITIES FOR PROBLEM SOLVING

Each craft project as it is presented should have only enough direction or procedure to assure some measure of success for even the slowest student. It must always have an "open end" that provides the condition for the child to discover things for himself and have full opportunity to develop his own technique and express himself in an individual manner. When a craft project is a good one, it quickly "takes over" and demands to be completed in its own way. If it doesn't "take over" it should perhaps be abandoned, for the outcome, if forced, will only be contrived and alien.

THE CRAFTS TEACHER AS ACTIVATOR

We tend to be highly critical of the teacher who simply will not allow the child to think for himself. This teacher gives specific directions or defines patterns that must be followed without deviation. Such teaching is deadly, but its antithesis is also of little value. The teacher who only hands out materials, then leaves children to "create" out of a vacuum, is surely not fulfilling his role, which is one of establishing a wholesome climate for creative work, providing good motivations, introducing sufficient orderly procedure to insure good foundations on which to work, and then permitting the child to use his own ideas in developing his project. The teacher should allow the child to work independently until he reaches his own stopping point, then try to stimulate the child's thinking by activating his passive knowledge so that he is able to go on to a new level of attainment that he would not have otherwise achieved. In effect this means that the teacher cannot be satisfied with everything that the child produces. Instead, he strives to see that the child continually wants to raise, and does, his level of achievement.

Naturally the range of achievement is wide in every group, so the teacher is forced to use a different set of values for each child. The teacher who seeks to have the children develop their creativeness to the fullest will constantly try different means to strive for the greatest possible achievement. For example, he may work with the children on ways to think up good ideas; he will open a lesson with a good warm-up discussion; he will try to recognize the children's creative ideas and encourage the divergent thinkers, those who take off in their own direction rather than focusing on the teacher's viewpoint. He will encourage the children to value their own ideas by allowing them to put ideas into action. Frequently a teacher comes to class with his own notion of what should result from a discussion or a lesson, and then, regardless of the creative ideas of the children, forces the group to conform to his ideas. This leads a child to feel insecure with his own ideas and become increasingly dependent upon the ideas of others. The teacher, like the child, must learn to value ideas and approaches that differ from his own. Although he must have high standards, he should not fix upon what he believes to be the ideal work, thus making children who do not create such masterpieces dissatisfied with their efforts. It is essential that each piece of work be viewed in the context in which it was made. Has this child made a gain? Does this show growth? Is it spontaneous? Is it personal? Is it skillful? Every child is a challenge, not just the gifted ones; every child can grow and make gains.

DIVERSITY IN CRAFTS TEACHING

We often speak of the differences between children but seldom think of the differences between teachers or schools. Each teacher and each school has assets and liabilities that affect the school's crafts program. Sometimes quantity or quality of materials may be the determining factor; sometimes it may be the teacher's own special areas of interest. Whatever the reasons, there is no school so poor nor any teacher so inadequate as to excuse the absence of art education from the school program. The arts and crafts program provides one of the very few opportunities for a total educational experience—one in which the child starts with an idea and is able to bring that idea into a tangible form. To begin, the teacher needs only the desire for a worthwhile program and the barest amount of materials. Often these materials can be scrap, if there is no other source. Given the opportunity, the child will supply the ideas and develop his own technique. It is reasonable to expect that the more one tries, the more proficient one can become as a crafts teacher. Therefore it is important to begin immediately and to try to grow in the same way we might expect each child to grow.

CRAFTS AS A LINK TO THE PAST

The history of man or any culture can be reconstructed through crafts. Man has always worked with his hands, using first the materials of nature and later products that he developed from those materials. In every land and at every period in history, man has worked with clay, fibers, wood, stone, and metal—the very same materials with which we work today. Many crafts that were produced as useful objects have lasted longer than their creators and have retained a quality that transcends time and function. These objects are recognized and valued for their own sake; as works of art.

In his earliest efforts for survival, man created tools and shelters, with concern only for their function. Very soon, however, he developed the aesthetic urge to pay attention to form and create ornamentation.

The art forms of other cultures can tell us a great deal about the people of those cultures. The teacher should recognize this fact and use it as a way of making each lesson or project more meaningful.

Almost any material or project presents the opportunity to establish cultural relationships. The child must be encouraged to create in the spirit of his times and with the materials of his culture, for to mimic or to try to recreate the past would be unreal. Nevertheless, a project can be much more exciting when, for example, working in clay modeling, the teacher comes prepared with photographs of the Hanawa horse or of a Chou bronze and stimulates the children's interest by discussing how the animal has been a favorite subject of artists throughout history, showing examples and drawing relationships among them. This means that the teacher has a learning experience before each major lesson and can share his learning. Teaching is neither giving nor getting; it is the great adventure of the human spirit, sharing.

CRAFTS FOR CHILDREN IN TODAY'S WORLD

Ours is a technological culture with decreasing emphasis on handwork and individual achievement. Many people work in industries that require such minute specialization that a worker may devote his entire career to one simple operation or act, such as putting a specific nut on a specific bolt hundreds of times a day, thousands of times a year, without ever feeling the relationship of his act to a total product. Some industries fabricate some parts in one place, some parts in another, and combine the parts in still another. This isolation and alienation of the worker from his job is repeated in business as well.

Crafts allow the individual to feel fulfilled, having to conceive his idea

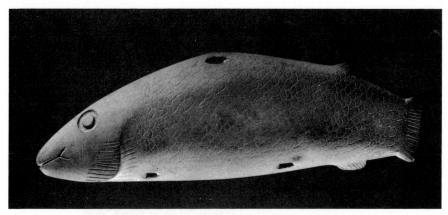

1-10

1-11

Figure 1-10. This neolithic stone carving of a fish was probably used as a weight or as a fishing lure. Carvings of this period have little detail and the stone representations are usually limited to contour. These simple techniques enabled the craftsmen of the Stone Age to create sculptures and drawings of an unusual aesthetic and dynamic quality, showing precise observation of natural life. (Hermitage Museum, Leningrad)

Figure 1-11. Most of the evidence of the Viking civilization and its art came from burial ships such as the one discovered at Oseberg, dated about 850 A.D. This was one of the richest prehistoric finds of northern Europe. It consisted of a ship about seventy feet in length, four sleighs including this one, a carriage, domestic utensils, jewelry, and weapons. These objects were richly carved in a variety of styles representing the distinctive art that flourished under the powerful Viking chiefs of the west coast of Norway and the Oslo Fjord. (Universitetets Oldsaksamling, Oslo)

1-12

1-13

initially, then carrying it through to completion. The craftsmen of the past went a step further on occasion, for they even designed, made, and ornamented the tools with which they carried out their ideas; they selected and picked reeds from the field with which to weave their baskets; sheared the sheep, spun the wool, made dyes from natural materials, dyed the wool, wove the fabric, then turned the fabric into garments. The completeness of a craftsman's work gives him a feeling of wholeness that is generally lacking in a technological society. A good crafts program brings the child face to face with himself as he applies his own ideas to a material, using tools that must respond to his will and skill, finally creating in tangible form a fresh combination of acts and ideas. He places himself in the position of receiving either the credit or the discredit for his product. He is not the cog, but the wheel itself.

The act of self-development takes place in experiences with simple tools and materials which allow the exploration of one's own potential. In complete involvement in a creative activity, the child comes to know himself. So much of life is group or organization centered that one can easily fall into the trap of having a group make most of his decisions for him, and thus find himself unprepared to solve even the most simple personal problems. While young, we learn the ways of self-renewal, or we never learn them at all. While young, we learn to deal with both persons and things. The small child comes to grips with his environment, one small part at a time, as he restructures it in his own way in crafts and art. Although the environment of the young child is enormous, the child has the amazing ability to simplify everything extraneous to his needs, and he has a perceptive appetite that can absorb almost limitless amounts of learning. Ideally, education should provide for a constant personal unfolding while the child absorbs and assimilates knowledge and enrichment from his environment. Thus the teacher's role is an important one, for he must provide the means for the child to interact with a rich environment, to discover and learn of his culture, cultures past, and cultures yet to be.

Figure 1-12. During the Bronze Age, 1,600 years before the birth of Christ, the great civilization of the Greeks began on the Aegean Islands as well as in Greece. Here, working in gold, an artist made two remarkable cups called the Vaphio Cups, which are still in perfect condition and which tell much about that civilization. The cups are made of beaten gold into which scenes of the capture of two great bulls have been raised by the method of repoussé. One scene shows the bull being trapped by a net; the other shows a bull being lured by a cow. The beautiful treatment is as easily appreciated today as it must have been more than 3,000 years ago. (The National Museum, Greece)

Figure 1-13. Before the Russian revolution, the population of Siberia was divided into the agricultural people of the east and south and the hunters, fisherman, and reindeer breeders of the north and far east. Bark and reindeer hide were widely used for food vessels, such as this birch bark container. Most Siberian art was limited to fur, leather, wood, bark, and bone. The natural environment and way of life of every group is reflected in its crafts. (Courtesy of Musée de L'Homme, Paris)

DESIGN AND ITS SOURCES

Designing is often considered that part of the creative process in which a fairly clear idea of the final art or craft product is achieved and documented through sketches, samples, or models. However, designing is rarely limited to a preliminary act; rather it is an ongoing, integral part of the whole process of creating, with design changes occurring up to the time the object is assumed to be complete.

Basically there are three main sources of design for crafts; nature, material, and function. Each of these depends, too, upon the imagination of the craftsman, and all of them may interrelate in any project. Nature is not to be copied, for an attempt to mirror nature would be neither successful nor valuable. Nature serves rather as a point of departure and a source of inspiration. Nature has served as the universal primary source of inspiration to the craftsman. To study the beautiful forms, textures, rhythms, and colors of nature can only help to increase children's sensitivity. Natural forms, such as seed pods, stones, shells, cones, leaves, and so forth, should be part of the school environment. Children should have frequent experiences in finding, touching, holding, and describing such objects. Nature may be used in direct interpretations in drawing and painting, but it will tend to become symbolic or abstract in crafts design.

A second source of design—function—dictates to some degree the shape and form an object is to take. A ceramic vase to hold flowers, for example, must have walls and a bottom to contain water. It must be covered with a glaze to keep it from leaking, and the wall must be thick enough to support its weight. Function follows a process of evolution, for the craftsman discovers modifications that are possible within the limits of structure. For example, a chair must have legs to support the seat, but they may be straight or curved, thick or thin, supported or unsupported, and so forth.

The last main source of design is the material to be worked with, which generally imposes its own limitations. For example, wood can be flexible when it is thin, rigid when thick, soft enough to carve, or so hard it can resist the sharpest

---

Figure 1-14. Most good craftsmen want to combine function and beauty. Not only must the product do the job for which it was designed, but it should also give aesthetic satisfaction to both the maker and the user. The design and treatment of this house key and keyhole make them transcend the ordinary. They bear the imprint of their maker's style and skill, and no other key and keyhole are quite the same. (Tiroler Volkskunstmuseum, Innsbruck)

Figure 1-15. Popular art forms, usually thought of as folk art, are evidence of the instinctive nature of art. Art activity has never been limited to any special elite group of individuals, but is carried on within most cultures by trained and untrained artists. The untrained are generally considered the folk artists. This cut paper decoration from Poland, made as a festival decoration, is typical of a craft handed down through a family. Mothers taught daughters, fathers taught sons. (Musée de L'Homme, Paris)

1-14

1-15

tool. It cannot be stretched or melted like glass. It will not rust like iron or dissolve in water like clay. In its way, the material suggests to the designer what may be done with it.

Nevertheless, the crafts teacher should keep in mind that no source of design exceeds the imaginative ability of the designer. No rules of design can extract anything exciting if the imagination of the child has not been aroused.

ART APPRECIATION

Art appreciation is having an enjoyable experience through seeing and liking an art object. Children learn to appreciate in the same way they learn other things. They learn to pound by pounding, to draw by drawing, to run by running, and to appreciate by seeing and understanding. Whatever the teacher does to help children increase their visual perception and understanding will lead toward appreciation. How successfully this can be done depends to a large extent upon the manner in which children are introduced to art and art objects. Care should be given to establishing a comfortable relationship, a familiarity—a friendship with art and art objects.

There are a variety of sophisticated theories on which to build a program in appreciation but for most teachers who lack special training in art and art history a simple, personal but very effective approach is possible when it is recognized that any experiences and information which increase the children's understanding of an art object will increase their potential for appreciating it.

The teacher cannot possibly provide all the information or experiences to fully understand everything about an art work but he can select key items of relevant information to satisfy basic curiosity and stimulate interest.

What is relevant information that might do this? Every object can be identified by a name—it is a ceramic vase, a stone carving, a portrait, an etching, a cathedral, a batik, a costume, or a reproduction of a painting. Each object was made by a process or series of processes similar or related to ones that the children use. A ceramic vase is made of clay, it may have been made on a potter's wheel, it was fired in a kiln, glazed, and refired. The processes are technical, scientific, and historical—all aspects of which can provide interesting and useful information. An Indian war shield was made of native materials and required simple tools. Its rawhide surface was painted with special symbols which had religious or mystical significance to the maker. To begin to understand the shield helps children to understand the meaning of art in the Indian's culture.

These simple examples suggest that appreciation uses the object of the children's attention as the stepping-off point toward deeper understanding and enjoyment. However, facts can also destroy the pleasure of the art experience if they are too abundant or if they interfere with the pleasure of viewing. There is no need to tell of Van Gogh's loss of an ear or to mention the most recent price of a Rembrandt.

Frequently the piece of art contains easily recognized objects or incidents which can be discussed by the children. They eagerly describe and interpret the lively horses of Remington and Degas, the scenes found in Currier and Ives lithographs, or the struggles of hunters and animals in the carvings of Eskimos. In talking about art objects, children learn to identify the objects—what is it? They learn to describe it, and they learn its meaning as they discover the source and the context from which it came. In learning about context, children are really engaging in the study of mankind. Art objects are among the most direct and tangible expressions of the philosophies and life styles of cultures. Every art object is replete with clues and questions—who made it? for what purpose? how was it made? how was it used? what was its significance? what qualities does it have to make it a work of art? The teacher who seizes upon this as a way of teaching discovers art as a stimulus for logical thinking, for analysis, for inquiry, and for simple research.

The effective teaching of art appreciation starts with the establishment of an environment in which an appreciative attitude is encouraged by the teacher. This premise carries the expectation that the teacher continually enlarges his repertoire of art experiences and finds increasing enjoyment in the many forms that art takes. Unusual knowledge and the study of art and craft objects are not as important as are openness and tolerance in such a teaching situation. The teacher needs to forget about trying to teach "good taste" and must control his special biases. What each child and each teacher likes or dislikes is a personal matter. It is possible to like art works that the experts judge to be poor and to dislike works that the experts acclaim as great. The important point for the teacher is to avoid quality judgments on art works based only on personal likes or dislikes. In selecting work to be viewed by children it is possible to find examples that are representative of the best of a particular period based upon the collective opinions of experts.

Children's tastes for art are conditioned by the culture in which they are raised. They never exist in a vacuum and are constantly affected by the styles and customs of their culture. Man's tastes have always been determined this way. What may have been elegant in one culture could have appeared ridiculous in another. For example, the elaborate costume of feathers, fur, and paint of an American Indian must have appeared beautiful to his tribe, but a Pilgrim father in such a costume would have appeared odd to his community. The fact that children's appetites for food, music, literature, art, and learning are largely determined in their earliest years suggests the importance of immersing them in art and making them aware of what is beautiful in life. If teachers do not attend to this no one else is likely to do so.

1-16

1-17

This means that art appreciation begins "where the children are" in their development, in their interests, and in their tastes. From such beginnings bridges are built to other art forms and other cultures. Children should learn to see and appreciate what is in their immediate environment regardless of its sparseness, and they should begin activities in which they can influence their environment. Art appreciation might begin with one daffodil in a peanut butter jar or it might begin by looking at the designs on a butterfly wing. What children see in their daily lives—houses, churches, pictures in magazines, flowers, weeds, motion pictures and slides, or pictures in the classroom are all part of the wall-less museum that the teacher must discover in the community. Art is everywhere—in the spirals of a seashell, in fabrics, in architecture, in sculpture, in books, in museums, in toys, and so on.

One of the best bridges to build in art appreciation is from children's work to the works of artists. Children and artists depend upon the same sources for inspiration—nature, people, fantasy, animals, conflict, etc. It is useful to introduce examples of artists who have chosen the same subject matter as the children are using. Sometimes the viewing of related art works may serve as a motivation toward self experiences by children. This does not mean copying, for quite the opposite is what

Figure 1-16. This gingerbread by John Philip Johnson is an example of the continued effort of the craftsman to maintain his identity. The craftsman of today finds himself sometimes alone in resisting the loss of identity brought about by mass production, technology, and the age of space and the computer. The craftsman continually strives to individualize, and to give meaning and value to every object of his creation, be it ever so simple or common. (Museum of Contemporary Crafts of the American Craftsmen's Council)

Figure 1-17. Even the common coin may be a work of art. These tetradrachmas are Athenian and date from the fifth century B.C. In addition to the many major art works that appeared in the classical period of Greek art, there were also many small statuettes and relief sculptures in bronze and in terra cotta. Many were found on the famous Acropolis of Athens, where they were placed as offerings to the gods. The most numerous of the small reliefs were coins, on which, to keep the money constant, the Greeks used the head of Athena and her owl and olive branch as a symbol. (Museum of Fine Arts, Boston)

Figure 1-18. *Like Father, Like Son* by Alma W. Lesch. Combining familiar items of clothing with other fabrics, the artist has composed a collage/stitchery which evokes a sense of nostalgia and wonderment. (Collection, Johnson Wax Company)

is desirable. A good experience in examining an art work leaves a greater residue than just a visual impression. It leaves a feeling and a meaning, both of which are part of creative production.

Art appreciation is an important part of childhood education and it should be part of a continuing and sustained program. In learning to see, to discriminate, to describe, and to know art, the child comes closer to fulfilling his potential. Art appreciation is a useful and practical approach to education in which all learning is enhanced through the increase in verbal skills, information, and aesthetic values. It also serves as a stimulus for the children's creative development.

2-1

two

MODELING AND SCULPTING

In the broadest sense, sculpture includes all representations in the round and in relief, achieved by modeling, carving, or constructing in materials. More specifically, sculpture implies mainly the carving of a solid material with sharp tools such as chisels, drills, burrs, or axes. Modeling is generally thought of as working with malleable or plastic materials using the hand or simple tools such as spatulas or modeling tools. There are almost no limits to the choice of materials for either of these processes.

Modeling and sculpting are among the oldest forms of man's expression. As early as prehistoric man found flat surfaces on which to scratch and draw, he found pliable clay with which to model figures. It was probably later when he first fashioned tools capable of carving wood or stone, but his first three-dimensional efforts are related to today's efforts, for the primary subjects of art have not changed much throughout the years. Only man's relation to his subject, his materials, and his techniques have changed.

Man was first inspired by the forms of nature that made up his environment—animals, birds, trees, and people. Only later, when he became interested in the mysteries of life, such as fertility, birth, and death, and became involved in mystical relationships to his environment, did he begin to develop abstract symbolism to express his feelings, desires, and beliefs. In many ways the traditional concept of sculpture is rapidly changing. The media for the adult sculptor now include all the materials and processes of modern production. There are sculptures of concrete, steel, glass, aluminum, and plastic. Sculptors use welding equipment, mechanical drills and presses, and many other kinds of construction equipment as legitimately as they use mallets and chisels. Color as in ancient Egypt is once again an integral component of many sculptures. Use of these newer media has, of course, resulted in sculptures that are less dependent on natural sources for

---

Figure 2-1. Bella Coola Figure, Northwest Coast Indians, British Columbia. The sculptures of the Northwest Coast Indians were closely connected to their everyday lives. They ranged in size from enormous cedar totem poles to miniature sculptures carved from bone or ivory. In style, the sculptures are noted for their simplification and their great power and expression. Because the work of these Indians was primarily of perishable wood, little remains that is earlier than the eighteenth century. (Statens Etnografiska Museum, Stockholm)

their inspiration. The child approaches modeling and sculpture in ways similar to those of all artists. He interprets his visual and tactile impressions of his environment, or he expresses in personal symbols his thoughts and feelings.

No art program can be complete unless it provides some opportunity for three-dimensional activities, such as modeling and sculpture. It is one thing to draw or paint one's experiences on a flat surface, but it is a far different experience to create three-dimensionally. Many children have great difficulty with two-dimensional media. The teacher may watch a child struggling indefinitely to draw a figure with legs crossed; the child might solve this problem immediately when working in clay, simply by lifting one leg and crossing it over the other. To work in new and different materials can itself be stimulating, and the limitations imposed by each new material cause the child to develop new ideas and to vary his mode of expression, experimenting, and inventing as he goes. Working in three dimensions can also provide opportunities for the child who is more interested in tactile than in visual sensations.

NONHARDENING MODELING CLAY

Probably the most widely used of the three-dimensional materials is the non-hardening type of clay known generally as plasticene or plastilene. This clay usually contains oil and glycerine, which keep it from hardening permanently. It is considerably less responsive than earth clays. This plastic modeling clay is popular because it is reusable and therefore economical. It can play an especially important role in the lower elementary grades, where the product is not of as lasting importance to the child as the process of creating it. In these lower grades, it is perfectly permissible for the teacher to re-form the children's products into lumps and use the clay over and over again. However, the teacher should do this without the children around, and only after they have lost interest in what they have created.

When working with clay with younger elementary children, the teacher should realize that there is no one right way of modeling. The older pottery or sculpture student must follow some processes (especially if products are to be fired); but small children should be encouraged to develop their own personal techniques. Unfortunately, many of our art-school-trained teachers were taught that the only right way to work with clay is to pull the features out of the whole —that is, to start with the solid lump of clay and to pull out the ears, and nose, press out the lips and eyebrows, and so forth. For some children this is an entirely satisfactory method of working, but others naturally make each part separately and join them together.

Because we stress the importance of being individual, we ought to recognize the fact that each person has his own way of working and can develop a technique

Figure 2-2. Here we see what one class did using the zoo as a subject for modeling. Begun with a wire armature made from a single piece of stovepipe wire bent and twisted into shape, they built up each figure with balls and masses of salt ceramic. The figure was pressed into final shape and smoothed with the fingertips before being dried and painted. The wire framework allowed a freedom of action almost unattainable with earth clay. (Photograph by Ed Leos)

only through his work. Some teachers hold a mistaken notion that, given the materials, the child will create freely by himself. This is a beautiful thought, but unfortunately it is not often true. In most cases it is up to the teacher to provide adequate stimulation or motivation based upon the child's own experiences. For example, the teacher might ask how to prepare a hotdog for eating. How is it held? How wide must the mouth be opened? How do you chew? Does it drip catsup or mustard on your face? Can you model yourself eating a hotdog? Some other stimulations for working in clay or plasticene might include: "I am catching a ball," "I am eating corn on the cob," "I am taking a nap after lunch," "I am petting my cat."

Since plasticene is soft and pliable, it requires no special tools or equipment; children can work on a piece of newspaper or old cardboard. It keeps best if stored in an airtight container. If the clay becomes old and hard, one can sometimes resoften it by warming and working glycerine into it.

COMMON EARTH CLAY

A second type of clay that is often used in schools is common earth clay. This can be purchased as dry powder to be mixed with water or moist and ready to use. This type of clay can be fired in a kiln, but as a rule it is permitted to harden by drying in air. Pieces can be softened by being soaked in water. This clay is about the same as that which the children might find in a clay bank near the school or along the edge of a stream, except that when purchased it is always in a refined, gravel-free state. Sometimes it contains certain materials to make it harden more permanently. Earth clay has definite limitations, in that it always shrinks during the drying process, preventing the use of any type of framework or armature inside the clay figures; built on a frame, the dry figure will generally break into many pieces. Therefore, the teacher working with ordinary clay must limit the modeling to rather compact, bulky figures without delicate appendages. However, such limitations are desirable, because they place before each child a new problem requiring a new solution.

If a kiln is available, it might be desirable to fire the works of the older children, but it is generally unwise to fire those of the very young. To fire the work of a child who is doing little more than "scribbling" in clay is to place undue emphasis upon the product. When using earth clay, it is permissible to allow the young child to paint his finished figure if he so desires. Teachers have no business developing "purist" attitudes about the art work of children, for anything that fosters sincere self-expression is desirable. Therefore, the painting of clay figures, which adult artists might shun, is acceptable with children.

If the teacher is working with powdered clay for the first time, he would do well to mix his clay with small amounts of water until it is a good consistency. A good consistency is one that allows the clay to be manipulated without cracking and yet be stiff enough the clay doesn't stick to the hands too much. A very pleasant and clean way to mix the clay is to put about a pound of powdered clay in a plastic bag, add a small amount of water, press out all the air, fasten the bag with a heavy rubber band, and give it to one of the children to knead. Kneading is itself often very enjoyable to young children, satisfying a kinesthetic desire. If the clay seems too dry, add a bit more water; if too moist, add some more dry clay. The teacher will soon discover his own formula for mixing clay and water to produce a good consistency. The clay will work best if allowed to age for several days after it has been kneaded. It can be stored for an extended period of time in the bag in which it was kneaded.

SALT CERAMIC

An excellent substitute for clay and plasticene that every teacher can make in his own kitchen or have made by the mothers of the boys and girls in his class is called *salt ceramic*. It is made by using one cup table salt, one half cup corn starch, and three quarters of a cup of cold water. These materials are mixed together in a double boiler placed over heat. The mixture is stirred constantly, and in about two to three minutes it becomes so thick that it follows the spoon in the stirring process. It quickly reaches a consistency similar to bread dough, and is then placed on a piece of wax paper or aluminum foil and allowed to cool. When it has cooled sufficiently to be handled, it is kneaded for several minutes, after which it is ready for use. If wrapped in wax paper or placed in plastic bags, it can be stored away for several days.

Salt ceramic will harden to the consistency of stone and is excellent for painting with any type of paint. It has several classroom advantages over clay. For one thing, it does not shrink when drying and therefore permits the use of any type of armature. Because it dries very hard, it is much more durable than ordinary unfired earth clay. Perhaps the feature that teachers like most is its cleanliness; when salt ceramic gets on the floor, it does not powder and get dust all over the school.

Through the use of the armature, a great variety of figures can be created with salt ceramic. If the children have been to the zoo or have seen a film or slides showing many types of wild animals, they may wish to create animals. Without an armature it would be quite difficult to make an animal like the giraffe, with its extremely long neck, or the gorilla, with its large upstretched arms. Using material

2-3

2-4

Figure 2-3. Sow (1928), wire sculpture by Alexander Calder. Although Calder is best known for his mobiles and stabiles, he is also a recognized printmaker and jeweler. Among his early works were simple linear drawings of animals, people, and circuses that are closely related to his humorous wire sculpture. (Collection, The Museum of Modern Art, New York. Gift of the artist)

Figure 2-4. These wax votive figures are about one foot high. Made by the Gautsch firm in Munich several centuries ago, they represent an early commercial trend in the ancient tradition of votive offerings. These offerings varied greatly—from the gold statuette that King Henry III had made of his queen and placed on the shrine of St. Edward at Westminster on their wedding day, to the full-length wax figure of Duke Alessandro de Medici modeled by Benvenuto Cellini for the Church of the Annunciation in Florence. (The Bayerisches Nationalmuseum, Munich)

of this sort often suggests group modeling, in which each child's product contributes a part. To use the zoo as an example, each child could model the part that interests him most. Perhaps the class could do a holiday scene, in which each child selects one of the major or minor figures to model. This sort of activity is especially good when children are ten to twelve years old, and can learn the meaning of cooperation. When the child sees a completed group modeling, he carries away a feeling of satisfaction for the completed project, fully realizing that what the group did as a whole he could never have done by himself.

WIRE SCULPTURE

Sculpturing need not be limited to solid forms, but can sometimes be created with just a piece of wire. It is very interesting to give each child about a yard's length of soft stovepipe wire and permit him to carry out his ideas with this material. The thinness and flexibility of the wire will send the child off exploring in entirely new directions. Wire sculpture is an especially desirable activity in, the upper elementary grades, where children are becoming conscious of body joints and bends, such as knees and elbows, in their drawing and painting. Wire allows them to bend figures at the knees, ankles, wrists, and elbows, and lends itself to a greater flexibility than any other material that they have used before. This is a sort of sculpturing that permits the figure to throw the ball and be quickly bent in time to be the catcher. Wire sculpture lends itself to a sort of action sketching in three dimensions, with a great consciousness and awareness of movement and, unconsciously, greater sensitivity.

Aluminum wire is about the easiest for boys and girls to use. This is very economical, extremely pliable, and noncorroding. The teacher can generally get a good supply of wire for sculpture and other activities simply by asking the newsboys in the class to save the wire that binds their bundles of newspapers together. As a rule, such a request to a group of elementary school boys brings an overwhelming response.

Wire sculptures are more attractive if they can be mounted upon a small piece of wood that the children can sand and wax, stain, or paint.

TOOTHPICK OR SODA STRAW SCULPTURE

Toothpick sculpture is another type of unit sculpture that is extremely fascinating to boys and girls in the upper elementary grades and in junior and senior high school. Probably no creative activity in which the child engages holds a greater fascination. Children become completely engrossed in building with toothpicks,

Figure 2-5. This magnificent slide in the children's playground in the Tivoli, Copenhagen, has been created with all the freshness and whimsy of a giant-sized sculpture. Children should be made aware of the beauty—or lack of it—in the functional forms around them. (Tivoli, Photograph by Else Tholstrup Gyldenkrane)

Figure 2-6. Every new material presents a completely new set of problems and possibilities. The use of a repeated form or element challenges the student to find new directions. Soda straws or toothpicks invite this kind of diversity since they cannot be treated like wire, clay, stone, or any of the other materials of sculpture. Nevertheless, this problem of limited possibilities will bring forth a great range of highly individualized treatments. (Photograph by Bill Coleman)

using model airplane cement for joining. They seem to find toothpicks a stimulus in themselves. It is exciting to watch the different methods with which children who are given these materials work. Some will begin simply with a triangle, develop it into a prism, and allow it to grow in all directions into a construction of planes and lines and, sometimes, closed forms.

It seems unimportant to the child as he builds to state what he is building or to be concerned with a conscious reason for building, other than that it seems to satisfy an urge to create something new. Some children who work with toothpicks seem concerned only with making something realistic and recognizable. This is permissible—and even desirable—since the limitations of the materials will help the child to develop new directions. The teacher may stimulate the children even further by giving them small bits of cellophane or colored paper that they can use to define a plane. Older students may use strips of thin, pliable wood, such as balsa, and combine it in structures with translucent tissue paper or cellophane.

The same sort of construction can be done with soda straws or colored tooth-picks. In working with airplane cement, it is a good idea to work on pieces of waxed paper, because cemented objects will not adhere to the waxed surface.

PARAFFIN OR WAX SCULPTURE

Paraffin is an extremely fine sculpting material that lends itself to ordinary class-room use and yet can be finished beautifully. Generally, paraffin is purchased in one-pound packages that consist of four quarter-pound blocks or slabs. The slabs can be used as they are at almost any grade level for very interesting relief carving, but some of the most interesting results come from fusing the four blocks into a solid mass, sometimes with the addition of a small amount of color provided by a wax crayon melted along with the paraffin.

It is not difficult to fuse the four blocks if a hot plate is available. The bottom of the waxed carton is carefully sealed with masking or gummed tape and placed in a container of cold water. Even better is a waxed or plastic-coated milk carton, which is less likely to leak than the paraffin box. One block is removed and melted and the remaining three separated slightly. The melted block is poured into the box, fusing the three remaining blocks. If the carton should leak slightly, the cold water will immediately harden the paraffin, thereby stopping the leak. Later, the carton is removed and the paraffin can be carved.

As is the case generally in sculpting, the shape of the block determines what is to be carved. Carving can be done with paring knives, wood-carving tools, or linoleum-carving tools. One good method is occasionally to have the children begin carving the paraffin block with no conscious plan, allowing the feel of the material to determine the outcome. Very often the paraffin lends itself to the creation of abstract sculptures, in which the children make beautiful forms that are as pleasant to handle as to view.

Paraffin is fairly sturdy, so it permits quite intricate cutting if the child desires to go into detail or is working in a realistic direction; but it is difficult, though not impossible, to repair. When all the cutting is complete, the child can smooth the paraffin by rubbing it with a rounded stick, such as a tongue depressor or an orange stick. He can bring it to an almost translucent polish by rubbing it with a stick, a smooth piece of cloth, or even the fingers.

Dropping a piece of wax crayon into the melted paraffin will sometimes cause the color to run through the block in a very irregular fashion. This in itself might suggest what shall be cut away and what shall remain. Sometimes the child sees in the color that flows through the block the image of what he wishes to create. Old wax candles or unbleached beeswax can be melted and added to the paraffin for interesting color. Occasionally, if the whole pound of paraffin is melted and poured back into the box, minute air bubbles will remain, bringing a rich appearance to the surface of the paraffin.

CONCRETE AND ZONOLITE SCULPTURE

In recent years, art teachers have developed one of the most interesting of all sculpting materials. This permanent material, extremely easy to make and to use in most classrooms, is made from a combination of cement and Zonolite, or Perlite. The latter are concrete aggregates made of mica, a very lightweight mineral substance also frequently advertised as an insulating material. Both the cement and Zonolite can be purchased from any lumberyard or home supply store.

For elementary level children, a good beginning mixture consists of four parts Zonolite to one part dry cement. An ordinary mop bucket or lard can serves very well as a mixing container. The Zonolite and cement are mixed together, and then enough water is added to make the mixture moist or fluid. It is well mixed, then poured into a small cardboard carton. It is a good idea to place the carton inside a larger carton on the first attempt, in case too much water has been added. The excess moisture may weaken the side walls of the inner box, causing them to break down. Newspapers wadded up between the walls of the two cartons will provide ample strength to keep the inner walls from collapsing. This mixture is allowed to harden for about twenty-four hours. The box is then removed, and the Zonolite-cement block can then be sawed into blocks of whatever size the teacher wishes. A good beginning size might be 5″ × 5″ × 8″ or 6″ × 6″ × 10″. The mixture can be carved with the simplest of tools—an ordinary kitchen or

2-7   2-8

Figure 2-7. Joansee of Augluk carved this stubby-legged Eskimo hunter. Much Eskimo art focuses on the human figure. Always bold, direct, and simple, it deals with the day-to-day struggle for survival, and most often shows men stalking game, hunting, fishing, or cleaning their kill. The Eskimo sees few living things, but he has trained himself to know well the creatures that surround him. He understands and respects the cohabitants of his world, and his art reflects these qualities. (The National Film Board of Canada. Photograph by Gar Lunney)

Figure 2-8. In this bronze sculpture, titled *Sailor and Guitar,* the artist, Jacques Lipchitz, introduces flat overlapping planes similar to those found in cubist painting of the same period. Even though Lipchitz consistently works in a variety of abstract and geometric styles, he strongly depends upon subjects drawn from his personal experience. (Albright-Knox Art Gallery, Buffalo, New York)

paring knife, an old hacksaw blade, a wood rasp, and an old screwdriver will provide all the tools needed to do a good job. The mixture is very light and is, therefore, extremely easy to carve.

When the student has created a sculpted form and it has been set aside to dry for several weeks, it will turn light gray, have a rocklike appearance, and be quite permanent. For junior and senior high school students, the same materials may be used and a finer texture created by cutting down on the quantity of Zonolite in the mixture. As the proportion of Zonolite is decreased, the density and hardness of the cast block increases. Of course, different tools will be required with the harder blocks. An inexpensive cold chisel and an ordinary hammer will serve for this type of carving.

Rarely does the classroom provide adequate facilities for each child to be carving at the same time. A good solution is to set up a carving table or a carving corner and allow one or two children to work at a time. Have each child bring in a cardboard carton and, when he is ready to start carving, fix the side walls of the carton so that he can work with his sculpture always inside the box; the dirt and chips that are cut away can remain in the box. When the piece is entirely finished, the box can be disposed of without any of the dirt ever reaching the classroom floor. This kind of procedure is almost essential if the classroom teacher desires to have the boys and girls work in carving plaster.

The procedure for plaster carving is about the same as that for Zonolite, except that the plaster creates a great deal more dirt and dust in the room and is extremely difficult to clean from the containers once it has set, whereas the container that has been used to mix Zonolite can easily be rinsed out and left in perfect condition. Plaster carving can be used most effectively in the junior and senior high school, but only under very controlled conditions.

RELIEF IN PLASTER

Plaster plaques or reliefs are very easily created in the upper elementary grades and junior high school. Each child can bring a small box in which to make his plaque. Plasticene is patted or rolled flat, and the entire bottom of the box is covered with layer about a half inch thick, on the surface of which the children can work their ideas out directly. They can make many exquisite shapes and textures by pressing a variety of objects into the soft clay. Dowel rods, buttons, natural materials, spool ends, large nailheads, keys, wire screening, and twigs are only a few of the possibilities. If the child's first idea doesn't work out satisfactorily, he can smooth the surface out again for a new start.

The teacher may wish to have the children work out their ideas first on paper with chalks or crayons. The teacher can explain the steps that follow more easily to children if he has prepared a sample for illustrative purposes and perhaps has a finished plaque from another class or even one that he has made himself.

The children begin by digging directly into the plasticene, using tools fashioned from tongue depressors split lengthwise. Into the plasticene they carve, deep in some spots, shallow in others, until they have expressed their ideas as fully and originally as possible in this material. The plasticene can then be given a very thin coat of petroleum jelly; however, this is not absolutely necessary, as there is already oil in the plasticene mixture. It does, however, prevent bits of plaster from adhering to the plasticene.

The next step involves the mixing of plaster of paris in a container, such as a plastic washbasin or mixing bowl, or a # 10 tin can. The plaster is poured onto the plasticene carving to a thickness of 1/2" to 3/4". While the plaster is still wet, the child can insert a loop of soft wire near the top of the back in order to hang the plaque. If the teacher encourages the children to jostle the boxes slightly without lifting them from the table while the plaster is still liquid, any air bubbles that might have been trapped in the plaster will rise, insuring a more uniform quality.

After the plaques have dried overnight, the boxes can be torn away and the plaques lifted away from the plasticene molds. Slight imperfections can be carefully carved away with an ordinary paring knife or smoothed with a small bit of sandpaper. After the plaques have dried for several days, they can be given a very light sanding to remove all traces of the petroleum jelly, which might offer some resistance on future painting operations. Now the plaques are ready for painting. Ordinary water paints, tempera paints, enamels, or oil-based paints are satisfactory for finishing this project.

If ordinary earth clay is readily available, it can be used just as effectively as plasticene. Unlike plasticene, which can be used over several work sessions, the earth clay should be carved and the plaster poured while it is still malleable. When the plaster has hardened sufficiently to pull it free from the clay, it may be necessary to take a moistened brush to wash away clay particles that still adhere to the plaster.

The teacher will find the children very excited about this project and wanting to do it another time.

SAND CASTING

Using the same principles as described for plaster relief, it is possible to make larger, but somewhat less refined, cast pieces of great charm. The main difference lies in the material in which the initial form is impressed or carved. First, some type of container made of flat wood, like the kind fresh cherries are packed in, lined with something to keep the sand from sifting through is needed (a plastic drycleaner's bag glued to the inside of the box will serve very well). A quantity of bank sand—a type that is fine and that packs firmly together when damp—is needed. Coarse granular beach sands are generally not too satisfactory. The sand is dampened and packed firmly in the box.

The carving is begun, using old spoons to remove the excess sand, and sticks and other objects to shape the desired form. The tips of the fingers are the most important tools, for they allow gentle tamping and sensitive shaping. Imaginative use of large, coarse textures, often in the form of a repeat, usually results in a more interesting piece.

When the form has been refined to the desired condition, plaster or plaster combined with Zonolite is mixed in a large container and poured into the scooped-

---

Figure 2-9. The lid of a shoe box, partly filled with firm clay, is the beginning of a relief carving. The child carries out his idea directly by removing and adding clay. When the relief mold is completed, the surface of the clay is brushed gently with oil or petroleum jelly and liquid plaster of paris is poured into the box. When the plaster is dry and hard, the box and mold are carefully removed from the plaster. Finally, the plaster is cleaned and sanded gently, and it may be painted.

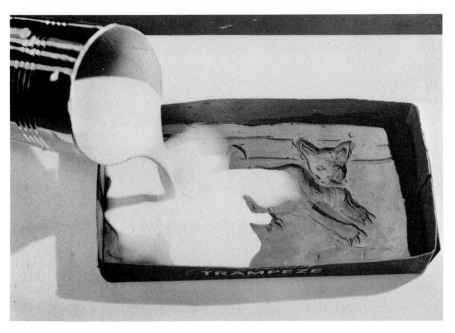

out form. Care should be used to pour the plaster gently, so that none of the form is washed away. A far more permanent casting can be made by using a dry, ready-mixed cement instead of the plaster. There are great advantages to this type of cast, as the cement is much easier to clean up and, if the container is to be retained for future use, to remove from the bucket or can in which it is mixed. If the casting is of unusual size, some fencing wire or metal rods can be inserted in the back as a reinforcing element during the pouring process. The concrete or cement casting will be able to withstand outdoor weather, whereas plaster ones will slowly deteriorate if left outdoors.

This activity is an especially good one for playgrounds and camps, where lots of sand is to be found and where size is no problem. Concrete, unlike plaster, needs several days to set up. If work is done outdoors, the cement should be dried slowly, remaining covered with damp cloths, and out of the sunlight. After several days, the form is removed, brushed, or washed. Any kind of device for hanging should be constructed and inserted in the back of the piece while it is in a moist or semifluid state, then allowed to harden in place.

RELIEF IN SOFT WOOD

If the classroom has space for working with tools, boys and girls in the middle and upper elementary grades can make attractive relief sculptures. These are worked out most successfully on pieces of soft wood, such as white pine, which is about three-quarters of an inch to one inch thick. The child develops his design or figure in the center of his board, including as few details as possible. He can sketch directly onto the surface of the board with a soft pencil, indicating by shading the areas to be cut away. It is a good practice, then, to fasten the board securely with "C" clamps to the surface of the workbench. This permits the child to concentrate entirely upon his project and does away with the frustrations that accompany shifting and sliding boards.

The youngster can then begin to work, using quarter-inch and half-inch wood gouges and a wooden mallet. With very little practice, he can learn to use these tools effectively. There is something very exciting in the process of carving wood, cutting away bit by bit and feeling the wood yield under the blows. If there is one especially sharp gouge for the classroom, it can be kept for hand finishing—that is, using the gouge in both hands without using the mallet. If in the end it seems necessary to sand the carving, the child should be allowed to do so. Finally, if staining is desired, the piece can be finished with ordinary paste wax mixed with a small amount of oil paint. There are oil waxes containing pigments that will provide fine, rich finishes. Several coats of wax and lots of polishing with a

2-10

2-11

Figure 2-10. This animal sculpture of the Magdalenian period is estimated to be 13,000–15,000 years old. The hunter of this period engraved and painted the animals of his environment with unusual accuracy and sensitivity, and in no sense do they seem primitive. One can only wonder about the meaning of such a sculpture to a hungry group of hunters. (Musée des Antiquities Nationales, Paris.)

Figure 2-11. Sand casting in concrete is not widely used by artists. This charming lion by Jarl Hesselbarth is an excellent example of the possibilities of a medium that requires only ordinary concrete and no special equipment or tools. (Courtesy of The Artist)

2-12

2-13   2-14

Figure 2-12. From a very few basic tools, which first were made of stone and later of metal, have evolved the great variety of tools of the craftsman and the artist. Every culture and age have made modifications to adapt them to the specific uses and materials of the time. This relief sculpture of a monk was carved on the end of a choir stall in the year 1284 in Pohlde, Germany, the monk working with tools almost identical to those found in any contemporary wood craftsman's studio. (Niedersachsische Landes Galerie, Hannover, Germany)

Figure 2-13. Soft wood or small branches are especially suitable for whittling. A small coping saw can simplify some of the larger cuts, which might be tedious with only a pocket knife. These figures, carved from branches and a small piece of lumbered pine, were done by campers who used only knives. Two of the figures were painted with enamels; the third was rubbed with floor wax until it had a rich luster. (Photograph by Ed Leos)

Figure 2-14. From about 1840 to 1900, the Indians of Canada's northwest coastal area carved totem poles that still stand in front of their homes as heraldic symbols of family or tribal history. This pole near Hazelton, British Columbia represents the human soul held in the hands of a legendary figure. Indian artists worked principally in three-dimensional representation and carried wood sculpture to a degree of perfection not seen elsewhere in North America. (The National Film Board of Canada)

soft cloth brings out a very rich luster in children's carvings. Boiled linseed oil mixed equally with turpentine can be applied to the raw wood for a rich, natural wood finish.

CARVING IN THE ROUND

Large solid chunks of balsa wood lend themselves to wood carvings by upper elementary and junior and senior high school students. Because balsa wood is so very soft, it can easily be cut, but it requires especially sharp cutting edges to prevent crushing. Successful small carvings can be done with nothing more than an X-acto knife. A fine-tooth coping saw blade can be used for the removal of large segments. The teacher should take time to demonstrate several methods of slicing out the portions of wood. With a small amount of practice, most children can learn to remove pieces of the balsa wood smoothly and are able to produce fine carvings. As in the case of simple relief carvings, children can either allow the cutting marks to remain or sand the finished product and give it a good finish with a coat of paste wax.

NEWSPAPER AND ZONOLITE MODELING

One can make an excellent modeling material by shredding newspaper and soaking it until it is very pulpy, then adding to this pulp a sizable quantity of wallpaper paste and quantities of dry Zonolite. This mixture can be used for building over an armature in the same way modeling clay would be used, but when it dries it has a very unusual textural quality quite unlike any other papier-mâché. It has a richness of color and requires no painting; it becomes permanently hard and quite strong.

Because of the ease of obtaining the ingredients for this modeling material, rather large pieces can be made at very small cost. Simple armatures can be made of sticks and wires fastened to wooden bases, or of tightly rolled coils of newspaper into which lengths of coathanger wire have been inserted. Children can create large bulky masses by wadding up large pieces of newspaper and tying them into place with string, then building on their surfaces with the papier-mâché/Zonolite mixture. It is desirable, when engaging in a project of this sort, to be sure that the armature is constructed well enough to hold up through the whole process. As a rule, a flat piece of board, such as plywood, which can serve as a base should be used to fasten the armature to prevent toppling. Time saved on later steps and the avoidance of disappointments and frustrations will more than make up for the few minutes spent developing a good foundation.

MOBILES

A mobile is a sculpture in space, characterized by movement. Alexander Calder, one of America's leading artists, has brought the mobile to a peak of perfection in recent years, and it is now an accepted art form very likely to endure. The making of mobiles in schools has become very popular. In many instances, however, mobiles are little more than collections of junk suspended by strings or wires, with no movement, or feeling of movement, and made with little sensitivity for the materials.

First, a mobile should move; second, it should balance. Mobiles are not easy to construct and are least successful in the lower elementary grades. Fifth-or sixth-grade children are more likely to succeed. To begin the mobile, it is necessary to string several pieces of wire tautly across the room at a height at which the children can work and to have available a variety of lightweight materials. Thin, springy wire; fast-drying airplane cement; lightweight cardboard; pieces of balsa wood; lightweight balls, such as Ping-Pong or small Christmas tree balls; and similar materials will work best. Finished mobiles should appear to float or dance gently through space. Therefore, the materials feel and look light. Here the selection and use of materials will help the children to learn that all materials cannot do all jobs and that a sensitive selection of materials is essential to good design. Good design in crafts results when the worker recognizes and respects the possibilities as well as the limitations of the materials with which he works and keeps in mind the effect he wishes to achieve.

Because balance is the essential design element, each portion must be balanced. Therefore, a mobile is most easily made by working from the bottom up, so that everything is in balance as it progresses. Two small elements are balanced with each other, perhaps on the ends of a thin wire, and this construction is hung by a silk or nylon thread. When it balances, it may be attached to a wire that has a counterweight, so that a perfect balance is attained at this level. This combination may be attached by means of a thread to an even larger wire, which is balanced by a similar combination, perhaps similar only in weight, not in appearance; and if the placement is good, all the elements will be able to turn freely without crashing into one another. On and on it goes, until the last, and generally largest, elements are reached at the top.

Fast-drying airplane cement is most useful, because it can easily attach pieces of cardboard or balsa wood to a piece of wire and will be firm in a matter of a few minutes. It is also good to put a dab of the cement anyplace at which a thread is attached to a wire to hold the thread firmly in place.

Mobiles are challenging and fun, but just like other crafts projects, really good mobiles require planning. When the so-called scrap materials are treated chaotically and insensitively, they remain scrap; but through sensitive handling, they can be transformed and "dematerialized" so that, for example, a bottle cap is no longer just a bottle cap but an element of design. It is important that we introduce projects of this nature as early as possible, so that the children can become aware of contemporary art forms. The teacher should make use of every opportunity to develop the children's awareness of the art in their world. Each craft lesson should also be a lesson in art appreciation, so that the children learn to see art in everything, and not only in museums.

WHITTLING

Whittling is a form of sculpture that is sometimes overlooked in our arts and crafts programs, but children can spend many satisfying hours whittling interesting figures and objects with a sharp pocket knife and a piece of soft, close-grained wood. The scrap box in the local lumberyard will provide enough interesting pieces of soft wood for a whole class of youngsters to do their sculpting with pocket knives. A simple project like whittling can provide many opportunities for creative problem solving in which the child must adapt his ideas or his desire to express ideas to the limitations of the wood and the pocket knife. The teacher should exercise care not to perpetuate the numerous stereotypes that exist in whittling. There are really only two basic rules: keep the ideas simple and original and the knives sharp.

REPOUSSÉ

Repoussé is relief modeling in thin metal. It has been an art form for thousands of years, and examples can be found in almost any culture where metal has been generally available. The earliest examples were often of gold, but any metals soft enough to shape have been used. Frequently repoussé was used to decorate utilitarian objects, such as armor for warriors, drinking cups, and so forth. For children to do repoussé successfully, they should be motivated to express something rather than merely to learn another process.

Work in metal foils involves a whole new set of problems and solutions. First, the manipulation of metal is unlike any other craft experience; second, the project is worked on from the reverse side of the metal. Metal foils, such as copper, aluminum, and brass, can be purchased from most school or art supply stores. They may be sold either by size or by weight; aluminum is the lightest, least expensive, and easiest to work with, though usually the least attractive when finished.

This project can begin with crayon drawings of whatever experience has

Figure 2-15. *Lobster Trap and Fish Tail* (1939) by Alexander Calder is a classic example of the mobile, which he developed as one of the most original art forms of twentieth century American art. It is, in a sense, a unique combination of science, engineering and art. The form moves gently from wind currents and is balanced with rhythmic precision. Calder now works in large monumental sheet metal forms, called stabiles. (Collection, The Museum of Modern Art, New York. Gift of the Advisory Committee)

2-16

2-17

2-18

been chosen to be illustrated, perhaps "playing with a pet" or "playing games at recess." The crayon drawings must be less detailed than a pencil drawing and may thus be more adaptable to the foil. When the drawings are ready and their aptness discussed by teacher and child, the piece of foil is placed directly beneath the drawing, which is traced over with a pencil point in order to leave an impression on the foil. Now the child turns the foil over and presses parts of the drawing out slowly and carefully by placing the foil on a stack of newspapers and rubbing over the part with a blunt stick. A tongue depressor split lengthwise makes an excellent tool for this purpose. Some areas may be pushed out quite far, while others remain fairly shallow. The depth of the depression depends upon the amount of pressure applied to the stick and the number of times the area is gone over. When the child has pushed the entire design out, he may turn the foil over and do some work on the top side. He may improve some areas by creating textured surfaces where they have not been pushed out or raised; he may do this by finding something to tamp with, such as a nailhead, pencil point, bobby pin, or other small item.

The back can be filled with soft modeling clay to prevent any raised surface from being pressed in if it is accidentally pushed or bumped. The finished foil can be fastened to a piece of plywood or wallboard; carpet tacks or gimp nails can be used to fasten it on wood. The child can polish the foil with steel wool and stain and wax the wood or paint the wallboard.

Children in the upper elementary grades and junior high school generally enjoy repoussé; but it is a process that frequently represents the worst in art and industrial arts education, for it is in repoussé that one sees the most stereotyped work, such as palm trees, sailing boats, jumping fish, bird dogs, and the like.

Figure 2-16. The weathervane is generally thought of as an American art form, but some date back to pre-Christian Greece. Some of the American weathervane makers were professional carpenters blacksmiths, but many were amateurs who carved and whittled for relaxation. These weathervanes reflected the life and attitudes of the people. For example, this humorous piece was used as a combination trademark-weathervane. It was made in about 1815 for the top of a butcher shop. (The Smithsonian Institution)

Figure 2-17. The Egyptian development of relief carving to one of its highest levels resulted mainly from the practice of covering surfaces with incised decoration. This small limestone from the Tomb of Ti in Saggara shows two vultures, one complete and the other incomplete, on a sculptor's teaching model. The sculptor has achieved a three-dimensional effect on an almost flat surface. (Cliché des Musées Nationaux, Versailles)

Figure 2-18. Much early American ornamental ironwork was executed by local blacksmiths. From iron they forged gates, hinges, latches, tools, and so on. Occasionally they were called upon to make an ornament like this Indian, which would have been used on a weathervane or fastened on a door. The grace and simplicity of this figure, made in Pennsylvania in the late eighteenth century, are reminiscent of the Egyptian slate pallets made almost 5,000 years earlier. (The Metropolitan Museum of Art, New York. Gift of Mrs. Robert W. deForest, 1933)

With proper motivation, students should be able to avoid stereotyped subject matter.

THE COPING SAW OR JIGSAW

With increased frequency, hand tools such as the coping saw and power jig saw are becoming part of the elementary classroom equipment. When they are used without thought, only stereotyped patterns result. Used thoughtfully, these tools are as capable as the brush or the crayon of creating original and imaginative forms.

Begin with simple contour drawings that have as little intricate detail as possible. The teacher must work with the children to help them understand the limitations of tools and equipment. A saw will not do what a pencil does (as the pencil cannot duplicate the brush); each tool is used to do what it does most effectively. That the saw cuts is obvious; the detail it can cut is to be discovered. Ideas and solutions come forth when they are called for, expected, and valued. So we begin with simple forms, representing the natural concepts that children have of people, animals, nature, and so on. Use of the saw soon shows what is possible and what is not.

Simple forms cut from plywood have thickness, and they can be arranged in space. As soon as space enters the discussion, we have entered the world of sculpture; and the student builds when he fastens three or four pieces on a flat wood base, standing apart from one another at different depths. In crafts, as in all teaching, we begin with simple activities and move on to the more and more complex ones.

IN CONCLUSION

There are many common materials for modeling and sculpting, as well as many fine local materials available to teachers in different parts of the country. In some areas, lava-type stones that are very satisfactory for carving can be found. In other areas, where scrap materials are readily available, teachers may find sizable scraps of foam glass used in large construction projects. Older children can make excellent sculptures from fire brick or sand cores from foundries where material of this sort is available. It is important that teachers be alert to find and use the materials available in their own localities. The most imaginative and creative programs begin at home, not in the art supply catalogs.

Figure 2-19. Working effectively with the materials of his environment, William Accorsi is not fettered by traditional concepts of sculpture. His buoyant, humorous sculptures range from toys assembled from found materials to large constructions, such as his Elephant House, used as a playground sliding board. (Museum of Contemporary Crafts of the American Craftsmen's Council)

3-1

three

PRINTING AND PRINTMAKING

A print is an original art work, the impression resulting from placing paper, fabric, or other flat materials in direct contact with another surface that has been treated with inks or paints. For example: one makes a woodblock by carving into a flat wood surface, then rolling ink onto the flat portions that remain. A piece of paper is placed against the inked surface, rubbed or pressed, then removed. The ink that adheres to the paper produces the print. One may also cut fine lines with a sharp tool or etch them with acid into the surface of a piece of zinc or copper. When the surface is covered with ink, then wiped clean, a deposit of ink remains below the surface in the lines. Soft, dampened paper is forced against the copper or zinc plate in a press under great pressure. The paper, pressed into the fine lines, picks up the ink deposited there and when pulled free of the copper or zinc plate contains a reverse impression in ink of the original cut or etched lines.

If one area of the arts were to be singled out for having made the greatest gain in attracting interest in recent years, it would probably be printmaking. It is certainly not one of the oldest arts, unless one stretches the imagination to include occasional stenciled forms created by the Romans, cylinder seals made by the Egyptians, or similar related prints. It was really not until the advent of paper that printmaking became a serious form of art. Then for hundreds of years it was limited to traditional methods, most of which were far too complicated to adapt to simple uses. Now with greatly improved materials, such as water-based inks, dry tempera paints that are easily made soluble, and inexpensive but good carving tools, printmaking has moved into the elementary classroom to stay. Paralleling the development of new tools has been the imaginative interpretation of the uses of the tools and the steady development of new processes as adaptations of or improvisations on old ones. Artist/printmakers have thus contributed greatly to the

Figure 3-1. *Saved Bird,* by Umetaro Azechi. This lovely print was made from carved wood blocks carefully hand inked to make impressions on rice paper. The artist was a poor farm boy who, while working in an engraving plant, scratched pictures onto lead plates and then printed them by inking the plates and pressing the paper against them. To his surprise, some of these were accepted in exhibitions. Encouraged, Azechi began to make wood block prints. His work has continued to reflect the simple, rustic quality for which he was first recognized. Today Azechi is one of Japan's most popular printmakers. (The Art Institute of Chicago)

development of the art in the classroom though children, unlike artists, are not concerned with making multiple copies of their work.

Processes that allow the child to reproduce the forms that he creates are important in the arts and crafts program. Small children can often be found making designs all over a sidewalk or wall merely by dipping their hands into mud and making a series of orderly (or sometimes chaotic) prints. Children at the beach create designs with sticks, sand pails, shovel handles, or even their feet in the soft, moist sand. This desire to design by reproducing one shape over and over seems natural with children in painting or drawing and should therefore be used. This unconscious designing can be seen in the drawing or painting processes where children repeat the same design over and over, thereby creating a pattern. After drawing a tree a number of times in one picture the child might say, "See, I have made a forest." (However, this desire to repeat one image should not be confused with the repetition of the emotionally and creatively blocked child who is able to conceive only one idea and present it over and over without variations.)

PRINTMAKING WITH STICKS AND FOUND OBJECTS

Perhaps the most widely used of these processes in the lower elementary grades is stick printing. For this process, children dip small blocks of wood of various sizes and shapes, sometimes capped with felt, into paints and press them onto a piece of paper. Stick printing sets can be purchased, but it is much more satisfying for the children to make sets of their own. A search of a wood scrap box plus a variety of bottle caps, jar lids, wooden spools, clothespins, and other objects will provide a more challenging set of instruments than the standard circles,

Figure 3-2. Jasper scarabs with cartouche, 13th Dynasty. The seal was most important in early civilizations before the invention of writing. The seal was an engraved stone that substituted for the signature or identification of a special person. Many of the early seals were in the form of cylinders or rollers, which were used to mark clay tablets. The scarab stamp seals, shown here, were used on papyrus documents. (The Metropolitan Museum of Art, Carnarvon Collection, Gift of Edward S. Harkness, 1926)

Figure 3-3. T'ai Tsung horse, Chinese rubbing, twentieth century. Rubbings have recently become especially popular as a means of recording historical items, such as the inscriptions on tombstones, cornerstones, and so on. As children, most of us learned the technique of rubbing by placing a coin beneath a piece of paper and rubbing over it with a soft pencil. The Chinese have used similar, though more refined, methods for many centuries. A damp sheet of rice paper over a carved or engraved surface is gently and carefully rubbed with a pad covered with a fine coat of ink. Unlike a relief print, where the ink is placed upon the carved surface, giving a mirror image on the paper, the rubbing is a facsimile of the surface. Work in rubbings can help children gain an awareness of textures, for almost any surface will lend itself to a rubbing. (The Metropolitan Museum of Art, New York. Seymour Fund, 1954)

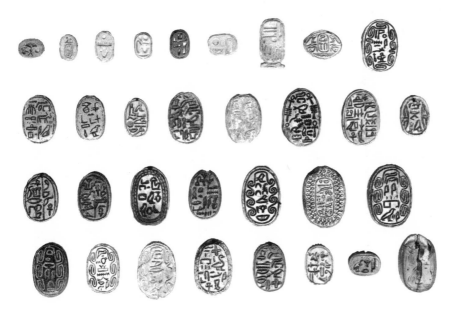

3-4

3-5

squares, and triangles the kits provide. The teacher may also wish to combine new shapes with those in a kit.

PRINTING WITH POTATOES AND CARROTS

Perhaps even more challenging is the child's own development of a design, using a vegetable as the printing tool. Some children may be able to bring a carrot, turnip, or potato; these are sliced in half, creating two smooth surfaces on which to design. Each surface may be cut with simple, dull tools: a paring knife will serve very well, and a melon baller is also useful. The child simply cuts away some parts of the smooth surface, leaving the remainder as the part that will print. Regardless of the child's ability to create "good" designs by adult standards, any design can be both effective and attractive if printed rhythmically and systematically. The teacher may stress the value of bringing order into the printing process, but without worrying too much about the design that the child creates. A good way to proceed with very small children is to have him "walk" the inked potato across the paper in even steps, and, when it gets to the other side, walk it back again. After he has made three or four lines, he will have created an even rhythm that will be orderly and pleasing.

Even at the earliest ages, children should begin to take pride in creating at the highest possible aesthetic level. Therefore, after they have printed a page of repeats in one color, preferably a light one, they can wipe the potato clean, select a second color, ink their vegetable again, and print over a portion of each of the original prints, thus creating multicolored prints in a uniform fashion. A variety of experiments of this kind will begin to open the door to the multitude of possibilities that awaits the inventive printer.

PRINTMAKING WITH MODELING CLAY (PLASTICENE)

One of the best and easiest printing surfaces for small children is ordinary oil-based modeling clay, commonly known as plasticene. Children can pound this

---

Figure 3-4. This boy is making a potato print. Having made a pad of soaked paper towels and covered it with tempera paints, he has then used this pad to ink his carved potato. He is now pressing the inked surface onto a sheet of newsprint, which is on top of several pieces of newspaper. This soft surface yields under the pressure, giving a sharp, clean print. (Photograph by Ed Leos)

Figure 3-5. *The Enchanted owl* (1960) by Kenojuak. Using a stone as his printing surface, Kenojuak, an Eskimo, carved this strangely beautiful owl and from it made many fine prints. Printmaking is a relatively new art to the Eskimo, but his adaptability has helped him to master it quickly. This print has the same simplicity found in the sealskin pictures made by Eskimo women and the same strength and boldness found in the carvings made by the men. (The National Film Board of Canada. Photograph by the West Baffin Eskimo Cooperative)

clay into small flat cakes about an inch thick, and carve on the flat surface directly with a bobby pin or small, pointed stick, removing portions of the clay. The ease in preparing a block for printing leads to very direct prints that perhaps resemble the drawings of the children more closely than other types of prints do. After the design is prepared, the surface can be smoothed slightly to remove any crumbs of clay that remain. Then the child can ink the surface with a rubber brayer (roller) just as he would ink a linoleum block and print by pressing the surface onto paper that is resting on a pad of newspaper. The newspaper should be of ten or twenty thicknesses, to insure good, clear prints.

Another method, probably preferable to the brayer method, is the use of the paint pad (see p. 61). This allows for much more rapid printing and a good deal less equipment. When the print is complete, the child can wash the paints from the surface of the modeling clay and return it to its storage place for future use. Some of the paint will remain, but it will not affect the usefulness of the clay.

PRINTMAKING WITH INNER TUBES

If a more controlled design is desired, one that is similar to a block print, the child can use an old inner tube, if he can find one. (One art materials manufacturer has already developed an excellent, but fairly expensive, product called printmakers' plate, which is similar to soft rubber with an adhesive backing. This cuts easily and is superior to the inner tube.) Cardboard can be used for this type of printing, but it is somewhat more difficult than rubber to cut.

The inner tube can be cut into pieces about 5″ square (or smaller or larger, depending upon the project). Each child is given a square. The children may sketch their ideas directly onto the inner tube with chalk and then cut out the designs with ordinary classroom scissors. The rubber design is then glued to blocks of scrap wood of any thickness. A child can print with this block in much the same way as he would with a rubber stamp or potato. If a cleaner, more accurate print is desired, especially in the upper elementary grades or the junior high school, the block print may be inked with block printing ink rolled on with a rubber brayer. The child may make a print can by placing the inked block on a piece of clean paper and standing on it, or by tapping it with a mallet or hammer. Either a water-based or an oil-based block printing ink is satisfactory.

The child can make an even more sensitive print by inking the block carefully, placing a sheet of onionskin tissue paper on top of the inked surface, then rubbing the paper with the tips of his fingers or the back of a wooden spoon. The image of the print shows through immediately, so the child can see whether or not he has made a complete impression. The teacher may wish to combine this inner tube method with some of the methods described later in this chapter.

PRINTING PADS

A good printing pad for the vegetable and stick prints can be made by using about twenty thicknesses of newspaper cut to about $9'' \times 12''$, saturated with water, and sprinkled with dry powder paints or moist tempera paints. The tips of the fingers can be used to mix the dry paint with the moisture on the pad until it is smooth and pasty enough to adhere to the potato or plasticene block. Using this, the child can press the potato or block against the pad, picking up color, then pressing it firmly against the paper on which he is printing. This process is repeated with each print.

PRINTMAKING WITH PAPER STENCILS

Still another way of making prints using a minimum of materials is working with paper stencils. Each child can be given four or five pieces of drawing paper about $4''$ square. Using his scissors, he can cut holes of various sizes and shapes into the center of each piece. (It is advisable to cut only one hole per piece.) When he has cut them, each child is given a cleansing tissue, a small piece of cotton, or a small patch of cloth, which is rubbed on a piece of colored chalk and picks up enough dust to stencil. One of the shapes is selected and placed upon the paper on which the design is to go. The child carefully rubs his tissue, making strokes from the stencil paper toward the center of the opening he has cut. He goes all around the edge of the opening until the paper beneath it has a good, clear print. The teacher may encourage the children to repeat this same shape across the paper, even making two or three rows. Now, using a new color, the child may combine a new shape with the first shape. To make two or three rows like this teaches the child the value of rhythm and repetition without the teacher's having to stress the words or to teach rules or principles.

The teacher may wish to have the children try all their shapes or create some new ones until they are able to decide on the combination they like best. Some of the children may even try to combine some of their shapes to create realistic forms; others will remain very happy creating abstractions. This chalk and stencil method can be used at any age level. The older children will make more complex stencils and use a greater number of colors. Junior and senior high school students can render quite complex and interesting holiday cards or program covers using this process. These students will probably cut their stencils with an X-acto knife or razor blade to insure more accurate, sharper edges.

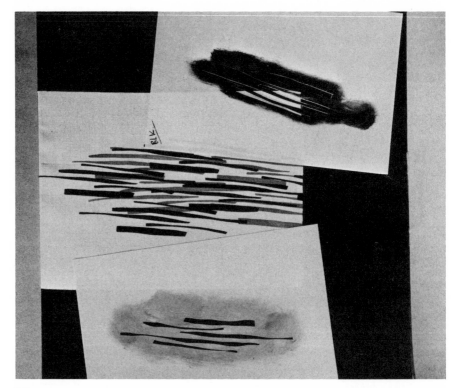

3-6a

3-6b

STENCILING WITH CRAYONS

This same stencil technique can be used with wax crayons in place of chalks, the crayons being rubbed directly onto the stencil. These stencils can be used very effectively on pieces of unbleached muslin or any other cotton material with a smooth surface. The children can make very attractive door and wall hangings, or even drapes or window curtains for the classroom. If the crayon is a good quality wax crayon, one can fix it semipermanently into the cloth by pressing it with a warm iron. It will survive a good number of careful washings with lukewarm water. The most interesting classrooms are those in which the children have a part in the planning and decorating. Nothing is so cold in appearance as a classroom with no evidence of the children who occupy it.

STENCILING PAINTS

Teachers in the middle and upper elementary grades or junior high school may wish to use the stencil method in a somewhat different manner. Most paints can be used for stenciling; they give a sharp and brilliant appearance to the stencil and lend themselves to greater detail.

With moist paints, the stencil process is essentially the same as with other media, with the exception that the paper from which the stencil is cut must be waterproof. Good waxed stencil papers are available commercially; these are not only waterproof but also transparent enough to permit good registry (correct placement of colors) where more than one color is being used. For the teacher who operates a program on a limited budget, however, there is an adequate substitute. Almost every school system, or some business establishment in town, has a mimeograph machine. On the back of every mimeograph stencil there is a heavy waxed paper that is torn off when the stencil is placed on the machine. This paper, which is normally thrown away, makes an excellent stencil paper for both water-based and oil-based paints.

With moist paints, one must use stiff bristle brushes. Those sold commercially are the best, but the teacher can make a substitute from a small enamel brush by carefully cutting the bristles with a razor blade about 3/4" below the ferrule, or metal band, that holds the bristles. By experimenting with the stencil brush and

---

Figure 3-6. The fabric shown in the lower photograph was printed from two waxed paper stencils using water-soluble textile paints. One stencil was cut for colored shapes and the second for black shapes. The pattern appears random except that the direction of all shapes is consistent and there has been an effort to balance printed and unprinted space on the fabric. In this case, the colored stencil was used first over the entire fabric, followed by the black stencil. (Photographs by Julius Shulman)

paint, the child can determine the correct amount of paint necessary and the best stroke for his design. He should be encouraged to work with a very dry brush that seems to be almost out of color, and to build up the color with numerous strokes rather than using one very moist stroke. If the brush is too moist, the color will seep under the edges of the stencil and spread unpleasantly, ruining the desired clean edge. Any type of water paints can be used for this sort of stenciling. Upper elementary grade and junior high school students will enjoy making greeting cards, programs, placemats for parties, and other projects that require a repetitive process.

PERMANENCE IN STENCILING

Having mastered the stencil method, the children may wish to put their newly discovered skills to work on a more permanent project. Excellent textile paints within the budget limitations of most schools are now available. These paints are so simple to use that no previous experience or special technical knowledge is necessary, and they are of such quality that they could be used successfully even in a commercial enterprise. The teacher who instructs her children carefully and encourages sound practices of economy and care for materials and equipment will find that a very small amount of paint will go far in textile painting. It is natural for children in the upper elementary grades and junior high school to be interested in clothing and decoration; therefore the classroom can serve excellently as a laboratory for experiments with problems designed to satisfy this interest. Using textile paint, children can print attractive window drapes, wall hangings, placemats, napkins, scarves, and other small items.

INDIVIDUALITY IN PRINTING

Teachers should make certain that children of all age levels develop their own designs when stenciling and block printing. There is always a danger that the child will copy stereotyped designs or even use ready-cut patterns that come in some sets of paints and thus limit his chances of developing creatively, through dependence on the ideas of others.

SPRAY PRINTING

Spray or spatter printing is a process that permits a wide variety of experiments in design. It is so fast and fascinating that a child can seldom be found who is not

Figure 3-7. *Children and Still Life* by Leonard Baskin. Leonard Baskin is one of the finest print-makers of the present day. His woodcuts range from large to very small, but each has the distinctly original style easily recognized as Baskin's. As a printmaker, he also works in wood engraving, and many of his excellent engravings have been used to illustrate books. (Courtesy of the National Gallery of Art, Washington, D.C.)

3-8

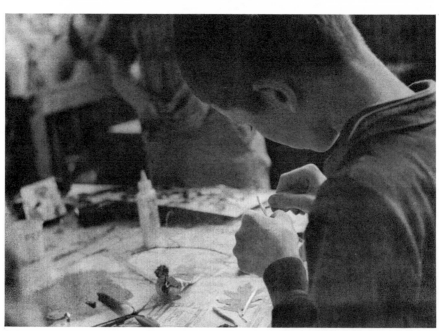

3-9

completely carried away by it. Only very simple equipment is needed to begin spatter painting.

Have several children bring old toothbrushes. Several will probably be enough for one room, as only one or two children work at a time on this project. Besides the toothbrush, the teacher needs only a small amount of water paint and some paper. The process is one of spraying paint with the toothbrush. A knife blade or other straight-edged object is gently pulled across the ends of the bristles, allowing the bristles to snap forward, thus throwing small particles of paint onto the paper. The child creates the design by placing small, flat objects or shapes upon the paper, thus preventing the spray from striking the paper and leaving the shapes free of paint spray and the rest of the paper covered with small spatters or flecks of paint. This technique, of course, has endless possibilities, in that one color may be superimposed on another and any variety of shapes can be used. Perhaps its widest use is with nature forms, for which the child gathers interestingly shaped leaves, twigs, weeds, grasses, and other objects.

Any vacant lot or field is an ideal hunting ground for the beautiful forms of nature. Finding beauty in nature is a project that in itself is valuable. When he has gathered them, the child takes some of his objects and arranges them on his paper. When he feels that he has an interesting arrangement, he places the paper on the floor, which has been covered with sheets of newspaper. He dips the toothbrush into some paint, shakes off the excess, and begins to spatter his design by carefully pulling a knife blade across the bristles of the brush, which has been aimed at the design. After a few trials, the child will learn just how much paint to use (and of what consistency), as well as the amount of pressure to put on the knife strokes. By experimenting, he can gain good control of the spray. After spraying his design, the child permits it to dry, then lifts away the natural shapes. He may find that one form has overlapped another, thus destroying the shapes of both; he may also find some areas that seem unnecessarily bare. He may begin to have some feeling for good composition without the teacher's ever having to mention the word.

Figure 3-8. Spatter painting makes use of the same principles as air-gun spraying. A portion of the paper is covered with another piece of paper, called the "mask," and paint is sprayed over the surface with the springy bristles of a toothbrush. When the paint is sufficiently dry, the mask is lifted off, exposing an unsprayed area shaped exactly like the mask. (Photograph by Ed Leos)

Figure 3-9. Projects that include items from nature help to increase the awareness of the beauty in the most commonplace things. Through careful examination and close contact with nature's handiwork, the child grows in sensitivity and appreciation. This child is preparing a surface for a graphite stick rubbing.

The natural forms should be only a beginning for the class, which should be encouraged to find all sorts of interesting shapes and forms in its environment in order to develop some completely abstract spatter paintings. If, however, some children wish to make a realistic painting, they should be permitted to do so. The limitations of the medium will cause them to deviate from their usual drawing and painting techniques.

After the class has begun spatter painting, some of the more inventive children will think of better ways of spattering, such as building a spatter box by covering the bottom of an old chalk or cigar box with a piece of window screening. They use this spatter box by rubbing a fingernail brush or very small scrubbing brush across the screening. Often the teacher will find a child who may seem limited in his creative ability according to the expected standards in drawing or painting, but who can think up a most ingenious spatter box. His creative efforts are being channeled into a new direction. Children do not always show creative abilities in the same ways; nor do these abilities develop at the same rate in all children.

OTHER POSSIBILITIES FOR PRINTMAKING

Children in the upper elementary grades or students in junior or senior high school can make excellent prints if the school system has any sort of press. They use a fairly heavy piece of cardboard, old poster board, or newsboard, which they cover with a very heavy coat of shellac. While the shellac is moist, they develop a design by placing pieces of string, seeds, rice, straw, burlap, weeds, or any other available materials on the shellac-covered cardboard. When these have become well set in the shellac, the children roll an inked brayer across the surface, touching all the raised parts and perhaps some of the flat areas. They then cover the inked design with a piece of drawing paper, place it in the press, and apply pressure. When the paper is withdrawn, it contains a printed impression of the design. A few experiments of this sort can open up many possibilities to the class and will serve as a point of departure for many diversified projects.

In combination with some of the other processes described in this chapter, this process can be used to print a background. For example, the child might casually drop a piece of wet cheesecloth onto the shellacked surface and permit it to dry just as it falls. When printed in the manner previously described, this will provide an excellent textural background. Often the cheesecloth or a piece of burlap will serve as a print itself if the arrangement is interesting. With this method, some children will attempt a representational print; but, as with previous processes, the limitations of press printing will provide new possibilities quite unlike those of

Figure 3-10. For printing larger fabrics, a blanket is placed on a smooth floor, then covered with the fabric to be printed. The fabric may be washed and pressed before printing to remove sizing or filler. The blocks are inked with oil-based inks to give a permanent print. Printing is carried out by pressing the block onto the fabric, carefully using the feet to exert equal weight on all portions of the block. (Photograph by Ed Leos)

drawing. Some children may make attempts at profiles using string, but string will provide other more satisfying results.

STRING AND ROLLER PRINTING

Another variation of printing may be made by using a brayer that is sticky with printing ink. If the child drops several pieces of string helter-skelter and runs the brayer slowly over them, the string will adhere to the brayer because of its stickiness. The brayer can then be run across the ink plate and paper. Each time the roller revolves, it will leave an impression of the string, thus creating and re-creating an interesting, dynamic design. This type of printing may be used for prints, as the basis for a future planned design, or as a background for block printing.

By experimenting, the teacher and children will find many variations of this type of printing. For example, scraps of tissue paper and thread or string may be dropped instead of the pieces of string.

AIRPLANE GLUE PRINTS

An attractive print can be made using an ordinary piece of window glass or a block of linoleum tile on which airplane glue or a cement of a similar type has been freely dripped directly from the tube. Using the clear glass, the children may want to make a sketch to place beneath the glass, which they will then follow with the drips from the cement tube. Some may prefer to work entirely spontaneously, developing the design as they drip the cement. After the cement sets for a day, the children ink the glass plate or tile in the same way that they would ink a block. The ink has a tendency to adhere to the raised surface of the cement and not adhere to the glass. A piece of a paper is placed over the plate and carefully rubbed with the back of a spoon or the rounded handle of a brush. When the paper is removed, the paper will bear an impression of the design created by the cement. When making prints from a piece of glass, one must exercise care to keep the glass on a smooth surface and not to place undue pressure on any one spot, which might cause it to break.

The child can get many variations from the glass plate by merely brushing the color on with a stiff brush, then placing his paper against the plate, rubbing the back of the paper with a hard, smooth object, and then pulling away his print. The piece of glass used in cement printing may be cleaned easily by being submerged in water for a short period, which will cause the cement to loosen and slip free of the glass.

MONOPRINTS

Making monoprints is a very exciting process that gives varied results. Perhaps the easiest method is to use a smooth, nonporous surface, such as window glass. Most hardware stores that sell window glass have a barrel of small pieces that they usually throw away. Pieces large enough for monoprinting can generally be obtained for the asking.

The teacher must use caution in handling these pieces, as the edges are extremely sharp. Much safer and every bit as good are pieces of formica or small aluminum cookie sheets. Using liquid tempera paints, or water-based block printing ink, the children drip various colors from matchsticks, toothpicks, or brush handles, creating designs or pictures on the glass. While the paints are wet, the child places a piece of paper over them and rubs it gently. When the paper is removed, it bears a brilliant impression, which is unpredictable and exciting. Sometimes two prints can be made one after the other, but never with exactly the same effect. The child can drip additional paints on the already used plate, or he may wish to wash his plate before making a new print.

In beginning monoprints, the teacher may wish to limit the children to a fairly small printing area, say $7'' \times 9''$ or $9'' \times 12''$. This will permit them to cut the drawing paper into smaller pieces and thus economize. Only each child's very best prints should be matted or mounted. Some children will make attempts at representation in monoprinting. They should be encouraged in such experiments, as they will make numerous color discoveries that can carry over into their later work.

In all the processes that have been described, the teacher should be watching for opportunities to use papers other than the ordinary drawing papers. The children should try some prints on newspapers, pages out of magazines, pieces of wallpaper, paper bags, wrapping paper, or any other types of paper. Imagine the interesting print a child might get by using an old road map as the background for a monoprint or blockprint. It is, in fact, a good project to have the children *find* as many kinds of paper as they can. The examination of a large variety of papers can make an worthwhile discussion period. In subsequent lessons the children can use some of their papers for drawing or painting projects.

Sometimes the very surface of a paper may suggest the picture that goes on it. The making of monoprints lends itself to all sorts of discoveries in color and texture that the children may use later in their other arts and crafts activities.

FINGERPAINT MONOPRINTS

Although fingerpainting will be discussed in some detail later, it should be noted that the most economical use of fingerpaint is with the monoprint. If the teacher

Figure 3-11. Monoprints depend a great deal upon the accidental merging of colors and forms, but many important discoveries in art come about initially through "accidents." By such experiments the child begins to see color and form possibilities, and he must work to master them so that they become a controlled part of his working vocabulary as a young artist. Sometimes children want simply to enjoy the spontaneous beauty of the monoprint; other times they use it as the basis of a painting. (Photograph by Ed Leos)

can obtain a small porcelain enamel work table for his room, the top will serve as the surface on which fingerpaintings are made directly. This means that purchasing expensive, clay-coated fingerpaint papers is unnecessary, for after a spontaneous fingerpainting has been executed, a sheet of ordinary newsprint can be placed over it and rubbed gently. A mirror image of the painting will be deposited on the newsprint, and the child can immediately begin painting again. In case an enameled-top table is not available, a sheet of formica about 24" × 30" or a piece of safety glass from a car window will make an excellent surface. Scrap formica is usually available in odd sizes from stores that install bathrooms or kitchens; safety glass comes from automobile junkyards. This monoprint process makes fingerpainting both easy and inexpensive.

AFTER PRINTING

Whenever children have been using a brayer and an inked plate for any of the printing processes, they can use the plate for some experiments before cleaning it. If the glass has been covered with block printing inks, a picture or design can be scratched through the ink surface, exposing lines of clear glass. A toothpick or other simple tool can be used for the scratching. Children can lay a sheet of paper over the glass plate, rub it lightly, then remove it. The paper will bear a reverse image of the picture that was scratched through the paint.

LINOLEUM AND WOOD BLOCK PRINTS

Linoleum and wood block printing are standard printmaking processes in almost all secondary schools, but they are also found in many good elementary education programs. Good carving tools are available from almost every school supply house. Linoleum cutting tools are less expensive than wood carving tools but are generally not satisfactory for carving wood. Linoleum tools have replaceable blades so that dull or broken blades are easily and quickly replaced. Both types of tools have U-shaped and V-shaped gouges of different sizes, a flat chisel, and a cutting knife. The U-gouges scoop out large areas, the V-gouges cut fine lines and detail, the chisel smooths flat areas, and the knife trims edges to obtain clear, sharp lines. A few well-cared-for sets of tools can serve typical classroom needs.

The most important part of printmaking is the development of a strong motivation, which provides the basis for personal expression. Too often, in the printmaking processes, the lessons are so directed to the use of tools that little attention is paid to what can be expressed. As a result printmaking processes often are used only at holiday seasons to make very trite and stereotyped cards. Instead, print-making should be used as a regular part of the art program at several different times each year. For example, after the children have been inspired by a film or a field trip in which they saw or experienced something significant to them, they might begin with a well-planned black and white sketch that can be adapted to a linoleum or wood block. After the child and teacher have discussed the sketch and its potential as a printing block, the sketch can be made directly on the wood or linoleum using a black marking pen. All the portions to be printed are darkened with the pen; all portions to be cut away are left unmarked.

The cutting is done on a simple jig (or bench hook) made of a flat board that has a strip of wood nailed across each end, with one strip nailed on one side of the board and the second strip to the other side. This jig is held against the table's edge by the one strip and the second strip holds the linoleum or woodblock firm while it is being cut. This simple device not only protects the desk and table tops but makes block carving safer and easier. The teacher should demonstrate a few types of cuts and stress safe practices and care of tools. He should emphasize the children's personal investigations and invention of techniques.

After the blocks are completed, they are ready for printing. Prepare one table for that purpose by covering it with newspapers and preparing an inking slab. The inking slab can be a sheet of formica or glass or a cookie sheet on which a small amount of water-based block printing ink has been squeezed. Roll the ink with a brayer until it has a "tacky" sound and feel. Prepare the block by rolling the brayer across it in both directions until the entire surface is evenly covered. Remove the block with the ink side up and carefully place a piece of paper larger than the block on the inked surface. Press it gently but firmly so that it adheres. Begin to rub the paper with the rounded back of a wooden spoon or similar smooth object until the entire surface has been evenly rubbed. Carefully lift one corner to see if the ink is adhering to the paper. If it needs additional rubbing, release the corner and continue to rub. Slowly lift the corner again and peel the paper free of the block. Check the print with the block to determine if additional carving is desirable.

Figure 3-12. This boy is cutting linoleum on a simple cutting board or bench hook constructed to fit the top of his desk. The board has a wooden strip at each end. One (hidden from view) fits over the edge of the desk and holds the board in place; the other helps to prevent the linoleum from slipping. The hand not being used is kept behind the cutting tool to avoid accidents. (Photograph by Ed Leos)

Figure 3-13. The first prints should serve as proofs in order to determine if additional cutting is necessary to achieve the best effect from the block. Water-based printing inks are easily removed from a block with water, but oil-based inks require either turpentine or paint thinners as solvents for removing the ink from blocks. Water-based inks are preferable for younger children or where clean-up is a problem with older children. (Photograph by Ed Leos)

3-12

3-13

Figure 3-14. Cat, Russian, nineteenth century. When the mechanization of printing brought an end to the hand illustration of books, woodcutters and engravers were engaged to decorate the printed pages. As early as the fifteenth century, ateliers, or workshop studios, were busy printing playing cards and pictures. In the woodcut, the artist first cuts away all portions of the block of wood except the parts that will appear in black. Because this will be a mirror image, he must plan his lettering in reverse. The block is then inked, with all the raised surfaces retaining the ink, and when it is covered with a sheet of paper or put through a press, an impression of the raised surfaces appears on the paper. This is called "relief printing." (Courtesy of The Art Institute of Chicago)

Figure 3-15. Twenty-two students worked on this linoleum block, each contributing his idea on a common topic. This required group planning and cooperation, both of which are essential to a happy life and neither of which can be learned through lessons and lectures. (Photograph by Ed Leos)

If it is, wipe the block clean with paper or cloth and return to cutting. If it needs no additional cutting, continue with the printing operation.

With a limited amount of wood or linoleum, several interesting projects are possible. One is to use a large sheet of linoleum on which each child draws a part of one common theme, such as "working in the garden." This can be handled like a painted or cut paper mural. When the drawings are in place, a group discussion will easily take care of empty or overcrowded spots or of elements that are too small or too large. Children have a fine intuitive feeling for good design, and group discussion will always aid in any cooperative project.

Once the plan is complete and agreed upon, each child can carve his portion. Finally a committee of several children can finish all unassigned areas and perhaps handle backgrounds. This small group will unify the whole design. With this type of print, the class can make draperies for the room; or each child can bring a piece of cloth, such as unbleached muslin, and with oil-based inks make a good wall hanging. An old blanket spread out on the floor makes a good printing surface. When inked, the block can be placed face down on the muslin, and the printer slowly puts his weight on every inch of the block to make a good, even print.

Another method is for the children to work on individual blocks, each child developing his own idea. Later each block is printed on one common paper or fabric in an orderly way to form a type of print mural.

Wood block and linoleum cutting and printing should allow the child to find a means of personal expression. The teaching of good procedures is also essential, for if the child cannot carry out his idea once he has developed it, he will gain nothing. If, on the other hand, nothing is stressed but the procedures of cutting and printing, the child may develop good technique but have few ideas. Time spent in thinking through a good motivation for such a project should produce better results.

To a large degree, the success of any printing process depends upon the kinds of surfaces on which prints are made. It is possible to make an ordinary black and white print remarkably pleasing by preparing unusual surfaces. Often it is impossible to have four or five colors of printing ink for all the children, so they can use

Figure 3-16. Linoleum cuts by African teenagers. Each of these young artists has achieved a very decorative result from his print using different techniques. One outlines his objects with single line cuts, and another cuts away most of the block, leaving only an outline around his objects; the two others depend upon larger masses of black and white to capture their ideas. Each block is successful and none is a stereotype.

Figure 3-17. *Agony in the Garden* by Ernest Barlach, German, 1870–1938. Barlach was concerned with the sufferings of humanity. His tormented figures, often beggars or outcasts, tend toward the grotesque. His style was made up of short incisive strokes, rather than the broad contrasts usually found in wood blocks. (Courtesy of the National Gallery of Art (Rosenwald Collection), Washington, D.C.)

3-16

3-17

one dark color. Each child can bring some old picture magazines or use colored construction or tissue paper to prepare backgrounds on which to print. The colors in advertisements are often much more subtle than those of construction paper. The child composes what he believes will be an effective multicolored background by pasting bits and pieces onto a plain sheet of paper to form the surface on which the prints are made. Astonishing results will come about both in the way color can enliven a print and in the child's color sensitivity.

When printing is finished, one can enhance prints by carefully mounting or matting them.

GRAINY WOOD BACKGROUNDS

One other interesting background that children might use is grainy wood. Each child should find a piece of soft, grainy wood, such as a piece of yellow pine or plywood. When he examines the wood, he will find that the grain is tougher than the wood surrounding it. This grain will remain firm when the soft part is scratched away with a knife, a large nail, or a wire brush. The process can be hastened if a torch is applied to the surface of the piece of wood, thus charring the whole surface. The soft areas between the grain become charred first and are then easy to remove. With the grain left standing, the board can be inked and printed and will serve as an excellent textural background for a block print of any sort.

SCREEN PRINTING IN A BOX

The inventiveness and resourcefulness of art teachers have slowly wrought changes and simplifications in the once highly difficult process of screen printing. Only a few years ago, the process challenged the best of technicians and was filled with frustrations. Today, many teachers use screen printing regularly as classroom work. The development of good water-soluble textile paint has made even textile printing simple enough for every school.

For the teacher who is trying to do screen printing with limited facilities and equipment, the following method may prove effective, especially if a large number of screens are to be used simultaneously.

Figure 3-18. *Old Stove,* linoleum print by Nancy Kupferman. Techniques vary considerably with the artist's intention. For this linoleum block a teenage artist chose a familiar subject, which she first sketched in black on a white surface. The transfer to linoleum for the purpose of cutting a printing surface required the development of techniques quite different from those used in the original drawing. (Courtesy of Nancy Kupferman)

The screen is constructed from a box about 10″ × 12″ × 2″. A cut is made about an inch from the edges to remove the center of the box (Figure 3-19a). A piece of inexpensive organdy is cut large enough to cover the outside of the box, including the vertical edges, and is stapled tightly to the box (Figure 3-19b). Wrinkles and creases must be avoided.

The box is then covered inside and out with brown kraft tape, leaving the center opening exposed (Figure 3-20c). The teacher should especially insist on neatness in this phase. After the box is well covered, it is shellacked heavily for waterproofing. Care should be exercised to avoid drops on the organdy. When the box is dry, the screen is ready for use.

In planning the first design, simplicity in color, detail, and composition is essential. Since color registry is a problem, color areas should not be so carefully defined that slight errors will be disturbing. Printing generally begins with the lightest color and ends with the darkest.

The child cuts the first stencil from mimeograph stencil backs, wax paper, or regular screen stencil paper; he makes it by cutting away only those parts that are to print (Figure 3-19d). He prepares the screen paint by mixing powdered soap with liquid tempera or with a good quality powder tempera and water. This should be stiff, of a consistency about like that of pudding (Figure 3-19e).

Now to the printing. Place a small stack of paper on the desk, and over this, the cut stencil and the screen box. Apply a good portion of the first color (about three or four heaping tablespoonfuls). With pressure, drag the paint across the screen with a small window squeegee or flat tongue depressor, making sure all areas are covered (Figure 3-19f). Lift the box from the stack of paper and you will find your print on the top sheet, while your stencil will have adhered to the bottom

3-19a

3-19b

3-19c

3-19d

3-19e

3-19f

3-19g

3-19h

of the box (Figure 3–20g), where it remains until the color run is complete. The squeegee process is repeated until a sufficient number of prints have been made.

Remove the stencil by peeling it free from the back of the box (Figure 3-19h). Wipe the screen as clear as possible with a dry cloth, followed by a damp cloth or sponge. Avoid soaking the box, since water diminishes its usefulness. It is impossible to remove all traces of color, but that is no problem.

This screen is now ready for a second stencil color. From this point on, the process is repeated as often as necessary to complete the design.

METAL FOIL PRINTS

The rapid changes in the packaging of foods have made a number of new materials available for printing. Among these are the heavy metal foils in which frozen goods are often packaged for baking. For example, if the budget cannot stand the expense of rolls of metal foil, the flat aluminum cake pans that frozen cakes come in can be used. The child places the flat foil on a thick newspaper and draws on it with a hard lead pencil, a ballpoint pen, or a pointed stick. The pressure of the drawing raises a line on the reverse side of the foil. The fact that the child draws with a small point permits details not possible with many elementary printmaking processes. Detailed drawings will satisfy some children much more than the larger, more simplified forms. When the drawing on the foil has been completed, the foil is stapled to a piece of cardboard with the raised side out. The plate is then ready for inking. A water-based printing ink is rolled onto the raised lines with a rubber brayer, the surface is covered with a sheet of paper, and the plate is pressed onto the paper under pressure, as with the linoleum block print, or rubbed like a mono print. When the paper is pulled free, the print that results is similar to a line drawing. As with all prints, the process can be repeated. The child can achieve numerous effects by combining this process with others previously mentioned.

A BEGINNING

Whatever the materials the teacher has to work with, he can work the reproductive processes into his program. It is up to the teacher to use the materials he has on hand and to find his own best technique. Limitations in materials should never be the excuse for lack of a good program, for often these very limitations stimulate the most interesting innovations and result in new and vital arts and crafts programs.

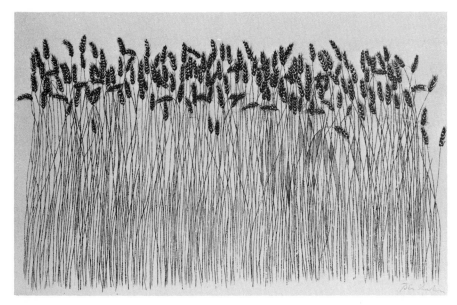

3-20

3-21

Figure 3-20. Wheat by Ben Shahn (1898–1969). Ben Shahn is known as an artist concerned with social and political issues. His distinctive, but constantly evolving, style along with his concern with critical issues have made him one of the major artists of this century. His silk-screen print or serigraph, a departure from his usual themes, demonstrates how the simplest subject can become a work of art when sensitively treated. (Courtesy of the National Gallery of Art, Washington, D. C.)

Figure 3-21. Using a large piece of heavy metal foil cut from the bottom of a frozen pastry container, the student carefully pressed a design into the surface. The embossed foil can serve as a printing surface or it may be mounted or matted as a repoussé. (Courtesy of Myrtll Kerr)

Figure 4-1. *Octopus and Diver from "20,000 Leagues Under the Sea",* ca. 1903, by Walter E. Deaves. The string marionnette is the most difficult type of puppet to make and to master. Some of the famous professional ones have such a range of movements that two people are required to manipulate all of the strings. (Courtesy of the Detroit Institute of Arts)

four

PUPPETS

In all parts of the world one can find puppets being used to provide entertainment. Perhaps this always has been so, for puppets seem to be as old as civilization. When the Twelfth Dynasty Egyptian tomb at Lisht was opened, four carved ivory dancing pygmies operated with strings were found among the treasures. In Greece, small figures with movable parts have been discovered in the ancient tombs. Plato and Aristotle, among others, mentioned figures manipulated by strings in their writing. It is thought that the first puppets of Greece were used by priests as part of their rituals. Later, as the rituals became more complicated, live actors replaced the puppets.

The modern puppet as we know it originated in Italy, where it was used in religious drama. As this type of drama became popular, the puppeteers traveled to nearby countries, and soon other countries adopted puppets for entertainment. It is known that at least one puppeteer, an Italian, was performing in London in the sixteenth century, and Shakespeare refers to puppets in several of his plays.

Europeans enjoyed both hand puppets and the classic string marionnettes that were used by itinerant entertainers and musicians. Their performances included satirical plays, stories of bravery and chivalry, religious dramas, and comedies. These programs attracted skilled writers and artists who designed and created puppets and marionnettes, costumes, and sets. The skill of these artists became so great that by the nineteenth century they were producing ballets, plays, and even entire operas.

In the early part of the twentieth century, the Punch and Judy show was still part of European and American tradition. With the increased interest in animated cartoons, motion pictures, and television, puppets declined in popularity. This trend has reversed itself somewhat, however, because of the adaptability of puppets to television. Once again children delight to the antics of the puppets of Bill Baird, George Latshaw, and others.

From about four basic types of puppets come innumerable variations. The first type, the hand puppet, is made to fit over the hand and arm. The head and arms of the puppet are moved by the fingers. Legs and feet are sometimes attached to the puppet figures, but they dangle and are seldom manipulated. There are many ways to construct a stage for hand puppets with a basic structure that is floorless and permits the puppeteer to work below the stage. Because of the simplicity of such stages, the scenery is ordinarily limited to a decorated backdrop.

A second puppet type is the rod puppet. These, like the hand puppets, are worked from below the stage opening. The puppet is constructed on a rigid rod and movement is created by one or more rods attached to the arms as well as the body. Some very large types, such as the life-size ones used in Japanese Bunraku (Kabuki drama adapted for puppets) require the puppeteer to be dressed completely in black while he works on stage with the puppet in view of the audience. The single rod puppet is very adaptable to school use at almost every age level.

A third type is the classic marionette, which is manipulated from above the stage by strings. This is the most difficult type to construct and to operate. There have been many remarkable marionettes whose agile movements were controlled by more than a dozen different strings. The marionette stage is a miniature of a regular theatrical stage with special scaffolding to allow the marionettes to be controlled from above the stage opening. In Europe, marionettes have had periods of popularity so great that they were recognized by the state and reviewed by the major theater critics of the day.

The shadow puppet is the final major type of puppet. It, like the first two types, is worked from below the stage opening. The figures are flat, two-dimensional cutouts fastened to thin wires or rods, which are used to create movements. These figures often are jointed so that they have movable arms, legs, or mouths. A light is placed behind a tautly stretched cloth onto which a simple scene has been painted. The puppet when held against the cloth from the lighted side appears as a silhouette to the audience. It is believed that shadow puppets originated in China as early as the eleventh century. The Chinese shadow puppets were con-

Figure 4-2. Guignol, French, nineteenth century. Some characters stand out in the history of the puppet theater, and Guignol is one of these. A jolly, carefree fellow with a wife named Madelon, he was modeled after real people whom his creator knew. Guignol always appeared clean-shaven and with a surprised look on his face. He kept turning up wherever anything important was happening, and was frequently found in the company of some pretty evil characters. Guignol was so popular that it became the practice to name hand puppet theaters after him. (Courtesy of the Detroit Institute of Arts)

Figure 4-3. *Toy Soldiers* by Edward "Nicholas" Nelson. The word marionette came into use in the seventeenth century. It refers to full-length jointed figures operated by strings from above. It is thought that the word may have come from the Venetian Festival of Mary, when street vendors sold "little Marys", miniature copies of the large processional figures of Mary. (Courtesy of the Detroit Institute of Arts)

Figure 4-4. Shadow puppets from "Fox Bewitchment". The best shadow puppets are found in Asia. The figures are mounted on a slender rod with jointed arms. Other rods are attached to the hands to control the movements. Usually made of buffalo hide, they are decorated with pierced designs to give them a translucent quality. In ancient times, women watched performances from the outside of the screen while the men sat behind the screen and watched the puppeteers operate the puppets. (Courtesy of the Detroit Institute of Arts)

4-2

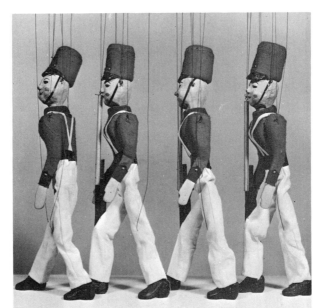

4-3

4-4

Figure 4-5. Punch and Judy, American, late nineteenth century. Throughout the nineteenth and early twentieth centuries, the hand puppets Punch and Judy were the main characters in many street performances in England and the United States. The plays were generally wild slapstick, with lots of action and noise to delight the audiences. Punch, descended from the famous Italian puppet Pulcinella, was a sometimes timid, sometimes cunning fellow. Millions of children throughout the world laughed at the antics of this pair and considered puppetry and "Punch-and-Judy" to be one and the same. (Courtesy of the Detroit Institute of Arts)

structed of animal skin, which gave a somewhat translucent quality to the figures. Many of the Oriental shadow puppets had removable heads, so that a simple head change produced a new character. The shadow puppets found their way from Asia to Europe where they also became popular. The evolution of this type of puppet seems inevitable; what child has not used his hands to cast shadows of animals, people, and what-have-you on the wall of his bedroom?

As an educational tool, puppets have become very widely accepted because of their value in helping children in personal development and the creative opportunities the building and operation of puppets provide. There is probably no greater thrill or sense of satisfaction than that which comes to the teacher who, through planning and effort, finds his pupils unfolding and revealing qualities that had lain dormant. Often these very qualities are not evident because the child lacks confidence in himself or is unable to communicate his thoughts and feelings for lack of the right medium. In puppetry, the teacher will find many possibilities for enriching most educational situations. Often, through the medium of the puppet, the child finds himself able to express thoughts, ideas, and feelings that he otherwise could not.

The puppet may serve as a therapeutic aid, but it has many other educational uses. Its wide range of uses and the large variety of types of puppets mean that their use is possible for most teachers in ordinary classroom situations. Puppetry is a teaching tool that can be used at any age level and can be modified to meet the physical and equipment limitations of even the poorest situations. There is no right way or wrong way to make puppets, but there may be a best way for each individual teacher. The teacher has to use the available materials and develop personal puppet techniques. It is good to know a number of ways to make puppets so that puppets can be used at different age levels without repeating puppet types and methods of approach.

To use puppets as a means of correlation of other studies such as reading or history is valuable, but correlation should never be allowed to become a limitation. Too often attempts at correlation are simply impositions upon rather than a natural outgrowth of a study unit.

PAPER BAG PUPPETS

Imagine a first-grade class in which the teacher desires to have the children express themselves freely and imaginatively. To begin the project, he has the children provide paper bags for themselves. With scissors, colored papers, paste, and paints or crayons, the children make faces on their bags. The teacher should be alert to stimulate the children to an awareness of the facial parts, perhaps encouraging experimentation with the papers for some three-dimensional effects. He should be ready to accept a wide variety of interpretations and should be careful to see that the puppet remains a product of the child's own imagination and experience.

At this age level, more emphasis should be placed on the *use* of the puppets than on the puppets themselves. After each child has completed his puppet, the teacher might suggest the beginning of a story, such as the following: "There is a little boy in our neighborhood who is about your age. He has a very bad habit of throwing stones at things. The other day he threw one over his back fence. Crash! Out came his neighbor, a very grumpy man. Out came his mother. The man began to speak to the boy; the mother spoke to the man. What do you think they said? What did the little boy say? Who would like to pretend to be the little boy, the man, the mother? That's fine, now come to the front of the room, put your puppet over your hand, and go behind the piano (or screen) and finish the play." At this point the children begin to express themselves. In this way the teacher can develop a play that will go on spontaneously for five minutes or so in which the children will adopt the suggested characters and identify with the problems of the little boy of the play. Teachers will frequently find that boys and girls who when called to the front of the class to read or talk can only giggle and laugh or are generally unable to express themselves may become quite at ease in a role in such a play. (However, puppetry is not a cure-all.) At this same age level, the teacher may want to develop in the children a greater feeling for group activities. To accomplish this, he may separate the children into groups of three, four, or five and have each group work out a play of its own.

STICK AND BAG PUPPETS

As a variation on bag puppets, the teacher may gather some sticks from the lumberyard or have one of the older students get some from the high school wood-shop scrap box. These should be about the size of yardsticks, but could be thicker or shorter. The rural teacher could cut twigs from a wooded area.

With this puppet, the child slips the bag over the stick and firmly stuffs it with wads of newspaper. He then ties the open end of the bag firmly to the stick; if a stapler is available, the bag can be stapled to the stick. He paints the head or makes a face with colored paper and paste, or uses crayons if they are the only available material. Perhaps a search of resources will uncover some scrap yarns, wood shavings, buttons, and so forth to decorate the puppet. Encourage the children to search for some new use for old, or seemingly useless, materials. This exploration in materials and ideas is basic to creative education.

Having completed a head on the stick, the children will want to make an

Figure 4-6. One of the most effective means of developing self-confidence in children is the open-stage performance. The puppet is not only the reason for speaking, but is also the means of self-expression. The otherwise shy child can say through the mouth of the puppet what he would like to be able to say in real life. Puppetry is not a cure-all for shyness, but used properly it is helpful in fostering healthy personality development. (Photograph by Ed Leos)

appropriate body. If no cardboard or oaktag is available, the body can be sketched on a piece of newspaper. The child can cut it out of about ten thicknesses of newspaper and staple, tape, or seal the edges with paste. He can then paint, crayon, or dress the body in colored papers. If the teacher is working on a limited budget, he can find an excellent supply of colored paper in the wallpaper books that the local paint, wallpaper, and decorator shops discard periodically as styles, prices, and lines change. This body can then be glued or stapled onto the stick. It will provide great pleasure if the child moves it as he talks. A good practice is for the children to give some movement with each word spoken.

This type of puppet lends itself to correlated projects, especially where children are studying other lands and peoples. It makes it possible for the children to design examples of the clothing worn by the people being studied, and lends itself to research by very young children. The middle or upper elementary grades are generally the best for this type of project, since children of this age have a high interest in clothing and dress.

MORE BAG PUPPETS

The common paper bag has endless possibilities for puppet making. In the upper elementary grades, a good project is to make puppets using nothing but paper bags. The children should bring in as many types and sizes of bags as they can find and plenty of newspapers for use in stuffing and for clothing. The bags are stuffed with wadded newspapers and stapled or glued shut. If staples are not available, the bags can be sewed shut with thread or yarn.

A child can start with his largest bag for the body. On top of it he may staple or sew a medium-sized bag to serve as the head. He may then take a long, thin bag and cut it in half lengthwise, making two long, thin bags. Of course he must paste, staple, or sew the open edges together so that they can be stuffed. These two bags can serve as arms and be attached to the "shoulders" of the largest bag. The child finds other bags to serve as legs, hands, or feet. If he is especially skillful, he may want to make joints at the knees and elbows. Sometimes little bags will serve as ears or a nose, or the child can modify the main bags to produce facial features. This type of puppet can simply be suspended by strings from a single stick, such as a yardstick, which can be jiggled to produce the effect of walking or moving.

Another child may find a long, thin bag that will serve as the body of an animal, and bags that he can use as legs, tails, ears, or a head. He may even make a lower jaw, so that his dog can bark or his lion bite.

Having made the main structures, the children can costume or decorate the puppets. Older age children are apt to be very inventive and to find many materials that they can bring from home to serve as the costumes. Children may come in with bits of felt from an old hat to serve as ears for a dog; they may find a piece of rope to serve as a tail for a horse, or a piece of old lace tablecloth or old window curtain for a fancy dress. This sort of puppet serves in dramatizing stories. Instead of being hidden behind a screen or stage, the puppeteers simply walk and move with their puppets in full view of the audience. This is significant in that the child no longer is protected by the stage. He is communicating in full view of his peers. The amazing part of such a performance is the fact that soon after the presentation begins, the audience becomes unaware of the children and becomes interested only in the puppets. Likewise, the children who operate the puppets soon lose any fear of the audience and identify only with the puppet.

CYLINDER PUPPETS

Another interesting and effective type of puppet is the cylinder or tube puppet. Children may begin with a piece of 9″ × 12″ or 12″ × 18″ drawing or construction paper and roll it into a cylinder. Where the ends meet, it is stapled or glued so that it holds its form. This tube then serves as the head of the puppet. Some children will make long, thin tubes; others will make short, squat ones. Some may even deviate from the cylinder and choose to make a cone shape or a modification of the cone shape. Such deviations should be encouraged.

Having made his basic shapes, the child should then be encouraged to decide what sort of person his tube might represent. Does it make him think of a pleasant person, a grouchy person, an old person? When he decides, he may proceed to make his puppet. Using paper, scissors, and paste, he develops a face. Since this type of puppet works best for the middle or upper elementary grades, it is a good plan for the teacher to encourage some three-dimensional experimentation with the cut paper on the puppet. Perhaps one child may discover a way to make the lips protrude from the face, whereas another may find a way to make the cheeks bulge, and still another may invent a new type of eyelid or eyelash. Still others may work out ways of making hair, mustaches, whiskers, ears, or tongues. Others may decide to put hats on their puppets. Some may make a bonnet; others may make hats with large, floppy brims; still others may make high silk hats. It is a wise teacher who encourages the children to experiment and to deviate from standard methods. It is in these variations and innovations that the children use their abilities to the utmost and that the craft is beginning to fulfill its most significant purposes.

To complete such a puppet, each child can make a small tube of construction

4-7

4-8

4-9

paper that fits snugly over his middle finger. This tube is fastened to the inside wall of the puppet head by means of staples, sticky paper, or glue. When the child slides his hand inside the head, with the finger firmly inserted in the smaller tube, the puppet is secure and easily managed. A body can be made of heavy construction paper, oaktag, newspapers, or whatever materials are readily accessible. It should be made bulky in order to conceal the child's arm. The stage may be the classroom piano, a large table tilted on end, or perhaps a large piece of wrapping paper stretched across a corner of the room.

This type of puppet is especially effective when the class is adapting a play from classroom reading. It is good because it requires few materials, because it is easy to make, and because the shapes of the heads place such limitations on the interpretation of the characters that the children are unable to copy stereotyped concepts. Imagine the ingenuity it will call forth from each child to make Little Red Riding Hood and the Wolf from cylinders rather than making them in a way in which they have always seen them, thus breaking the stereotypes so often found when familiar characters are used.

VARIETY IN PUPPETS

Excellent puppets can be made very rapidly on perfectly flat surfaces. A picnic plate will serve as a good form on which to make the head of a two-dimensional puppet. These can be made using some of the same methods described previously, such as fastening the picnic plate to a stick and making a body of construction paper or oaktag. Children may also try to invent finger puppets built on simple tubes and decorated with colored papers and scrap materials.

For variations with younger children, a teacher may want to use fruits, styrofoam Christmas balls, or vegetables as the heads for puppets. For example, a

---

Figure 4-7. Rumpelstiltskin, by George Latshaw. The hand puppet is made to fit the puppeteer's hand: its parts operated by the fingers. Sometimes it is also known as a fist puppet or a glove puppet. Parts like legs, wings, and tails are often added, but they are usually not controlled. The puppeteer depends upon larger movements to emphasize effects. In the same way, the larger visual effects are of greater importance than details. (Courtesy of the Detroit Institute of Arts)

Figure 4-8. A potato long past its point of usefulness was impaled on a wooden clothespin and decorated with paper curls, pipe cleaners, thumbtacks and bottle caps. The sprouts continued to grow, forming a most unusual hair or headpiece.

Figure 4-9. Wilbur, from "Wilbur and the Giant" by George Latshaw. This unusual puppet was fashioned from a variety of common kitchen utensils. Mr. Latshaw, its creator, is one of the most imaginative puppeteers, and makes all of the puppets with which he performs. He continually seeks new and unusual materials and interpretations to keep his characters fresh and appealing. (Courtesy of George Latshaw Puppets, Cleveland)

withered potato or a sour apple with a clothespin inserted to hold it by would serve as an excellent foundation for a puppet. The children can bring in buttons, pins, or old costume jewelry to serve as facial parts. When apples are ripe country or suburban children may find cornsilk or grasses to serve as hair and whiskers. Some bits of cloth or an old stocking will make an excellent dress. Sometimes puppets are made from discarded light bulbs or rubber balls using similar methods. It goes without saying, of course, that great care must be taken with light bulbs or with any glass used by children.

Teachers should take these materials and find several ways to make them work rather than believe that there is only one right way. If the teacher cannot find ways to use them, the children surely can, and will, if given the opportunity. It is important to insure that each child have a good measure of success. Failure can become habitual. It is wise for the teacher, when embarking upon a project of some duration, to begin with some directed suggestions, so that each child builds a good basic structure on which to create. The child should learn to listen and to follow directions. In each craft activity, the teacher should be able to find a good balance between directed and creative activities.

A LIVELY HAND PUPPET

In the following puppet activities, the teacher should proceed slowly and see that each child keeps up with directions until the basic structure is complete. This project involves a three-dimensional fist or hand puppet that will serve at any level beyond the third grade and which allows such a range of expression that the poorest student will make a successful puppet, while the most gifted can go as far as his creative abilities allow. The materials should be ready to work with at the start so that the class can proceed rapidly and smoothly through the initial stages.

Have prepared for each child a small container with some water in it, a small bundle of newspapers, about one yard of brown sticky paper (gummed kraft tape), a piece of construction paper about 3″ × 9″, and a pair of scissors. Have the children cut their kraft paper into strips 1/2″ × 12″. When this is done, take the piece of construction paper and wrap it around the index finger on the hand that the child will use to operate the puppet. This should be wrapped snugly, and yet loosely enough that it can be removed easily. Wrap the tube with a piece of gummed kraft paper that has been moistened by a small wad of newspaper dipped into the water. Small bits of kraft tape can be turned over the ends to keep the tube from telescoping when the finger is withdrawn. The child then crumples a double sheet of newspaper by starting at one corner and slowly forming it into a ball about the size of a baseball. This is packed like a snowball so that it stays

Figure 4-10. Puppet making can be an especially good project for two children to work on together. Construction paper is wrapped around the index finger to make a tube, then sealed with gummed kraft tape. A ball of crumpled newspaper is fastened to the tube, and strips of tape are wrapped around it and run down the sides to secure the connection. Then the features and limbs are added with paper and paste. (Photograph by Ed Leos)

4-11

4-12

4-13

4-14

round and compact. One of the foot-long pieces of gummed kraft paper is then moistened and the ball of newspaper placed in the center. The child perches the ball on an end of the tube, and the free ends of the tape are brought down and stuck onto the tube. This process is repeated, with the sticky paper going over different parts until the ball is secure on top of the tube. It may still wobble slightly, but the wobbling will disappear in subsequent steps. A quantity of wall-paper paste is put into each child's container, and his desk is covered with several sheets of newspaper. The children tear pieces of newspaper into small strips, which they dip into the paste and then apply carefully to the ball and tube. About three layers of these strips are applied to the entire surface. The very slow pupil may not be able to go much beyond this point. But having reached this point, he will have a sufficiently good form. Features such as nose, mouth, eyes, and ears can be painted on it to create a perfectly satisfactory puppet. At this point, however, the truly creative part of the puppet making begins.

Now the children must make some decisions regarding their puppets. Who or what is it? Will he be kindly or mean, young or old, animal or person, fantastic or realistic? Children reach these decisions easily. Occasionally they should make puppets with no special characters in mind. The variety of characters that appears will serve as a stimulation for developing new and interesting stories and plays.

The child builds up the major features by placing larger wads of paper wher-ever necessary. For example, if the puppet is to be a chipmunk with large, bulgy cheeks, two wads of paper can be placed in the proper position and fastened down with some strips of newspaper and paste and built up until the cheeks puff out just the way the child thinks they should. From this point on, the puppet making is a modeling process in which each of the features is built up with small bits of

---

Figure 4-11. Although the shadow puppet is thought of as the dominant type of the Orient, other types, such as the marionette or string puppet, are frequently used. This one from Ceylon has a beautifully carved head of wood. (The Smithsonian Institution)

Figure 4-12. Using a new paper bag still in a folded position, the child inserts his hand carefully so that his fingers bend over the folded bag bottom. By gently opening and closing his hand, he can get the illusion of a mouth opening and closing. Paper, felt, and yarn quickly transform the bag into a character that talks, growls, or barks.

Figure 4-13. This puppet is constructed on a brown paper bag containing a paper wad to form the head. The bag, tied beneath the head, is squeezed together and taped so it can be easily held. The arms are not manipulated and the effect of the puppet is obtained through large exaggerated movements.

Figure 4-14. This simple marionette has a wooden frame and leather hinges. It can be strung with a thread for the head and for each arm and leg. Or it can be operated with only three threads— one for the head and one on each shoulder. For puppets like these, large, jerky limb movements are usually more effective than small, detailed ones.

paper soaked in the paste until they are soft and pliable. Some children will add an additional large ball of paper to form a snout or long nose to make a pig or goat. Others may cut large floppy ears from eight or ten thicknesses of paper. These are strengthened by dipping them into the paste so that the edges become saturated and sealed. When the features are completed, the puppets are put away to dry.

DRYING PUPPETS

There are a number of good ways to dry the puppets. One method is to build a simple rack by drilling holes into a board and inserting short dowel rods. One can make a simpler rack by pounding large nails into a board and resting each puppet head over a nail. This keeps the forms from being flattened or from sticking to another surface. A convenient method is to suspend them by a string attached to the neck. Hang the heads from the underside of the chalk trough beneath the blackboard. When these have dried overnight, they become rigid and hard and have very solid surfaces.

The children may work on these puppets in subsequent lessons if necessary, but it is important not to allow any of the craft projects to cover too long a time, for the interest span of children is limited. Once their interest span has been exceeded, it is difficult and unwise to try to continue a project. In the elementary school, it takes an exceptionally strong stimulation to hold the interest of children for more than four or five lesson periods. However, each group is different, and teachers may find wide variance in attention span.

ENLIVENING PUPPETS

When the heads have dried, they are ready to paint. A can of water-based or rubber-based interior wall paint makes a good undercoating on which to put the tempera paints and makes the classroom paints go much further. Usually one of the children can find a partially used can that he can bring from home. However, an undercoat is not essential, and puppet heads can be painted with any kind of paint. If the school budget does not provide dry powder paint or tempera paint, the teacher may be surprised by the variety and quantity of paints that the children can bring in from their toolsheds and basements. Naturally the water-based paints are best, since with them no special solvent is necessary to clean the brushes after use.

At the same time they are making the heads, the boys and girls can roll tubes to fit the thumb and middle finger. These will serve as the arms and hands of the puppet. There are many ways in which the hands can be made. A simple way is to

4-15

4-16

Figure 4-15. *Bird in the Hand beats the Bush* by George Latshaw. Using ordinary fabric gloves, Mr. Latshaw has created a series of delightful puppets which are very animated and very expressive. Occasionally a puppeteer may use only a bare fist which has facial features added with stage makeup. (Courtesy of George Latshaw Puppets, Cleveland)

Figure 4-16. In addition to the satisfaction of making a puppet, the child should have the opportunity to project even more of himself in the experience through performing. It is in this phase that children are able to express freely and openly some of the things which are difficult to express in the classroom. This is not to suggest that puppets are a catharsis; instead, they become a tool for easier and more open expression. The range of ideas and emotions are almost limitless in a puppet play, in which children are encouraged to give full play to their imaginations and their fantasies. The play or show culminates the activity thus eliminating the fragmented or partial experience, so commonplace in education. (Photograph by Ed Leos)

form a hand of soft, thin wire and attach it to the tube, covering the wire with bits of paper and paste. Another method is to cut a hand from a piece of cardboard and fasten it to the tube. If the child wishes, he may build the hand up with bits of paper and paste. For some puppets that represent animals, the ends of the tubes may be closed with wads of paper and become paws. When the head and hands are completed, the children should be encouraged to bring in pieces of cloth, old materials, needles, and thread from home to sew a costume. The costume should be made as simple as possible, but always large enough so that the hand can easily be inserted into it, with the index finger going into the neck tube and the middle finger and thumb into the hand tubes.

DRAMATIZING WITH PUPPETS

Children who make puppets of this type will want to put on performances that require some planning and practice. Simple stages can be made of large cardboard cartons from grocery stores. One can make a very simple stage by stretching kraft wrapping paper diagonally across a corner of a room and cutting a hole into the center of it to serve as the stage opening. A second piece can be similarly stretched, but about 18″ behind the first. This will serve as the backdrop, and on it the children can paint scenery. They can also make the scenery of colored paper. For a real dramatic performance, the room can be darkened and the stage lighted with a spotlight or an ordinary lamp directed into the stage opening. Children old enough to make these puppets should also be inspired to develop their own plays. The plays are always more spontaneous if the children are not held rigidly to a script, but are permitted to express themselves freely within a general framework. After several rehearsals, they will put on a polished performance with no script in hand. Puppets of this sort are fine for school parties or for entertaining parents on special occasions.

A VARIATION

Some teachers prefer to use this type of puppet by having the children first model the head from a plastic clay, then cover it with petroleum jelly and finally build up successive layers of paper and paste until the head is about five or six coats thick. When the layers have dried sufficiently, the head is cut in half with a razor blade and the plastic clay is removed. Then the edges are sealed together with bits of paper and paste, thus making a very light but strong head with which to work. This method takes a great deal more time and effort than that previously described, it produces stiffer, more rigid puppet heads than other methods, and provides accuracy and detail where desired.

STOCKING PUPPETS

A very nice type of string marionette can be made from a woman's cotton stocking. This puppet can also serve as a cuddly doll. The children are asked to bring in a stocking and some cotton batting or other material suitable for stuffing (for example, an old nylon stocking that has been shredded with scissors), a needle, and some yarn with which to sew. The child cuts off the foot of the stocking at the ankle, leaving only the long tube. The stocking is then turned inside out and one end tied shut with a piece of string. It is again turned right side out. A wad of cotton batting is stuffed into the stocking to form the shape of a head. The stocking is wrapped beneath the head with a piece of yarn or string to form the neck. More batting is stuffed into the stocking to form the upper part of the body. The stocking is wrapped below this to form the waist, and again it is stuffed to form the lower half of the body; but this time the child sews across the stocking below the body. With his scissors, the child cuts the remainder of the stocking lengthwise to form the two legs, and these in turn are sewed up each side so that they may be stuffed. They are stuffed down to the knee. If there are marbles available, one should be inserted at the knee and the leg wrapped above and below it to give a flexible joint. If marbles are not available, a smooth pebble will serve. The rest of the leg is stuffed and the botton sewed shut. The foot of the stocking is then split lengthwise and the open edges sewed shut to be used as arms. Half the arm may be stuffed and tied off, a marble or pebble inserted, and the arm finished in the same manner as the leg. This will form the elbow joint and make the arm very floppy. The arm is then sewed fast to the shoulder of the puppet. When the second arm is attached, the main part of the puppet is then complete. Bits of felt from old hats may be used to form feet or shoes; bits of light-colored cloth may be used for gloves or hands. The feet and hands should be weighted if the figure is to be used as a puppet. The faces can be made by embroidering the features with yarn or by sewing on buttons or appliquéing pieces of felt or cloth. Hair can be made of pieces of yarn or other scrap material.

The child can costume the doll in whatever manner he wishes. A search through mother's ragbag may reveal enough interesting pieces of cloth to make adequate costumes. If the dolls are to be used as puppets, they are suspended from a crossbar by means of heavy black thread attached at the knees, shoulders, hands, and the top of the head. The mechanism should be kept as simple as possible, so that movement can be obtained with a minimum of technical knowhow.

five

DRAWING AND PAINTING

One may wonder why a section on drawing and painting appears in the middle of a crafts book. The answer is simple. Art and crafts are inseparable. Both call upon the same personal resources; the same feelings and thoughts are expressed in both; both require the same skill and perseverance. Neither is of greater value than the other.

Drawing and painting certainly are among the most natural ways in which the child, or man for that matter, expresses his ideas and feelings. This is because they are direct, often immediate, ways of making a tangible record of the images the person perceives and his interpretations of them. What individuals perceive is reported in the visual arts in many ways. It seems quite clear that no two individuals ever perceive in exactly the same way: that is what makes art exciting. The differences among individuals become evident through their personal interpretations, techniques, and responses. It is obvious that there is no single "right" response. It may well be that things are "right" only when they are personal interpretations, not dependent on the concepts of others.

Man has apparently always had a need to express what he feels, for as early as there is any record of man, there is some evidence of his interpretation of his environment through pictures. The earliest examples are found inside caves, protected for thousands of years from the elements. These tell the same story that modern man's paintings tell, the story of man and his relationship to his environment. The diversity of ways in which this theme has been handled over the thousands of years that man has expressed himself is almost beyond description. It would indeed require a lifetime of study to comprehend even a small segment of it. In these records of man—his drawings and paintings—the history of civilization is recorded, for the highest aspirations, deepest feelings, most dramatic actions, strongest external forces, mysteries of life and death, religious beliefs, joys and sorrows, good and bad, all make up this recorded, continuous story.

Man is still expressing these very same things, often in a visual language that

Figure 5-1. Much of what children learn is absorbed from their environment. Environments that are rich as a result of careful planning afford the opportunity for continuous learning and the development of individual sensitivities. This rich painting of flying buzzards by an eight-year-old resulted from viewing a science film. (Courtesy of *Everyday Art Magazine*)

5-2

5-3

Figure 5-2. Sioux shield with Thunderbird and wavy lines symbolizing Thunder. The Sioux Indian's art was restricted, owing to his nomadic way of life. He decorated only objects easily carried on his person, such as this circular war shield of hard rawhide covered with tanned deerskin. On this he painted a symbolic emblem, which probably came from a dream or vision and through which he hoped to gain strength and protection from some supernatural force. (Courtesy of the Denver Art Museum)

Figure 5-3. *Vite Aerea* (Wind Screw) by Leonardo Da Vinci and a model based on the drawing. Science and art have always been related in many ways, and science and technology have long served as a source of objects of art interest. Sometimes the object has aesthetic qualities that interest the artist, but here Leonardo provided first a sketch of unusual aesthetic value, which served as a plan for the model constructed later by others. (Courtesy Museo Nazionale Della Scienza e della Tecnica, Milan)

seems remote and unclear to the viewer, and sometimes in forms that are obvious, trite, and shallow. The artist does not follow the mainstream of man's perception; he moves ahead, in directions that often seem hard to follow. We either place value on children's moving, thinking, and acting in divergent ways or we block the potential of children who seek to develop in divergent ways. Drawing and painting, like the crafts, offer a most unusual educational opportunity for this kind of development.

What do artists and children express in drawing and painting? First, they paint about themselves: what they look like, what they do, and how they feel. Then they paint about themselves and others: what we look like, and what we do together. They paint and draw about games and sports, their social activities, their schools, their families; about the places where they live and work and play. Their pictures tell where they have been or where they would like to go, imaginary places far away. They tell us who is important—the policeman, politician, minister, teacher, neighbor—and what it is like to be rich or poor, frightened, hungry, loving or hating, rejoicing or despairing. They draw in a style of precise visual reality or in the vaguest of abstractions. But always the basic theme is the same— man and his relation to his environment.

One of the things that each teacher should do is help build in the children a desire to persevere and to master the use of certain tools. This means that drawing and painting cannot be once a year or once in a lifetime activities. The children should have regular working periods in drawing and painting *at every grade level*, and the problems should increase in difficulty and in the length of time allowed. Children resist only threatening experiences, never attractive ones. When children resist drawing or painting, or any activity for that matter, it generally is because they feel threatened by personal inadequacies that will lead to products unsatisfactory to themselves, their peers, or their teacher. This need not be, for the young child expresses himself without any conscious fears. Fears are introduced only by the application of unreasonable standards. Regular drawing and painting activity, with regular open and free discussion and some guidance by a mature, sensitive adult, will help eliminate most of these problems.

Drawing is the basis for practically every pictorial activity; the techniques of drawing vary with each child and with the child's intention. Before the child reaches school age he makes many attempts at drawing, commonly referred to as scribbles. When he reaches school this urge to express, to record, to communicate, to experience should be broadened and deepened. Although there is no simple formula to help the teacher meet this basic need, he should recognize that art education may contribute uniquely to its fulfillment. Human experience is expressed in the visual forms of art in ways unparalleled in life and other forms of education.

There are several broad areas of concern that enable teachers to provide more adequately for meeting the aesthetic and creative needs of children. First, the art program should include a productive portion in which children are helped to develop attitudes and skills that will enable them to create visual and plastic forms for expression and for the communication of their ideas, feelings, and imagination. Productive skills make visual and plastic expression possible, but they can only be developed through sound, direct, and well thought out creative classroom experiences.

Second, there is a cultural portion of the program, in which children develop a broader understanding of art works and their evolution, development, and function in human history. To understand such forms, the teacher must provide experiences that help explain the significance of art forms in the context of the culture within which they were created. The child who begins to understand the visual arts and their significance to human culture has a means not only for viewing that culture more accurately, but for understanding his own culture and himself as well. Such experiences might be in the form of pictures, stories, films, slides, research, field trips, or discussions.

Still another concern is the development of the child's critical facilities, those visual and intellectual sensibilities that make it possible for the child to appreciate the forms of art. This, in effect, means providing the kinds of experience that increase visual and tactile sensitivity. This sensitivity does not automatically

---

Figure 5-4. *Hinterglasbilder,* by unknown Yugoslavian peasant artist. In many European peasant homes, shrines, and wayside chapels, one can find many fine examples of hinterglasbilder, or painting on glass. Usually selecting subject matter from religious stories, the artists create these charming paintings on sheets of glass. They are usually viewed from the opposite side. (The Bayerisches National Museum, Munich)

Figure 5-5. *Boy on a Tricycle* by Stephen Gray, age 5. Using a minimum of detail and with no concern for the adult concept of space, this child has achieved clearly and with great feeling and charm an image of himself on his bicycle.   (From the Ninth Annual Exhibit of British Children's Art, 1958.)

Figure 5-6. This second-century encaustic painting was found in Fayum, Egypt. Encaustic ("burning in") is a process in which heat is used to keep the wax in which the pigments are mixed in a fluid state. Such pictures were baked to seal them permanently against the ravages of time. The Fayum portraits were painted during an individual's life to be placed over his mummified body after death. They were painted with heavy wax, put on very quickly, and later smoothed with a heated metal tool. There are many such portraits to be found in today's museums. They are remarkably well preserved and must be almost as fresh in color as they were when painted. (Reproduced courtesy of the Metropolitan Museum of Art, New York. Rogers Fund, 1909)

Figure 5-7. *Woman with Cats* (1955), by Alexander Calder. Although Calder is best known for his metal mobiles and stabiles, he is nonetheless a highly skilled graphic artist. His drawings have the same simplicity of form as his early wire figures. Calder's work contains an element of humor and playfulness and has the same honesty and directness so often found in the drawings of children. (Reproduced courtesy of The Art Institute of Chicago. Gift of Mr. Frank B. Hubachek)

5-4

5-5

5-6

5-7

5-8

5-9

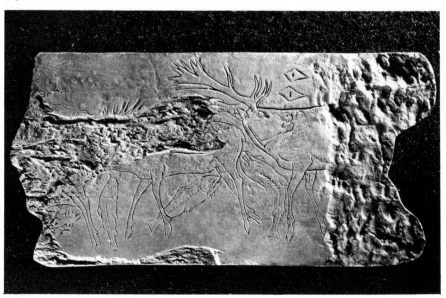

develop with maturity; rather it must be developed through planned experiences. One learns to see by looking and knowing how to look and what to look for. Therefore, many guided looking and touching experiences are useful and should be supplemented by ample open intelligent and unbiased discussion about what is being examined. This implies the use of plenty of support material, such as pictures, films, and slides for art instruction, and the development of evaluation and discussion techniques compatible with the productive portion of the program.

A good program ought to put great emphasis on the nurture of children's abilities and pay attention to providing the kind of environment that helps shape abilities and attitudes, as well as providing information and guidance. The development of the child is never the automatic consequence of growing older. In short, the teacher must be the key to the aesthetic development of children.

Children come to school to learn, and most of them eagerly assimilate anything that is offered. This is why art teaching is not left to chance. Teachers must plan lessons in which learning is possible and expected. At the same time, experiences in drawing and painting must be kept interesting and exciting. Wax crayons and sheets of $12'' \times 18''$ paper at every lesson cannot long hold a group's interest. A variety of materials and problems are required to give the children the chance to explore, discover, invent, and learn. Enough time and enough varied experiences should be allowed for mastery of the tools and materials, for it is only through their mastery that children will desire to work again. Children want to hide their failures and parade their successes.

MATERIALS FOR DRAWING AND PAINTING

What the child intends to do will largely determine the materials he needs and the techniques he will employ. A drawing with clear contours and small detail may require a pencil, pen, or nylon-tipped pen on smooth paper. Another drawing,

Figure 5-8. *Still Life* by Georges Braque, 1882–1963. Braque was one of the pioneers of cubism and, along with Picasso, invented *papier colles* and collages that combined painted forms with added bits of paper and other materials. Throughout his lifetime he continually increased in inventiveness and was a recognized master of drawing and design as well as painting. This painting has freshness and spontaneity and with great economy makes its statement. (Courtesy of the Art Institute of Chicago. Gift of Robert Allerton)

Figure 5-9. Impression of engraving around a deer antler of fish with lozenges, from Lorthet, Hautes-Pyrenees, France, Magdalenia period. Life in the Magdalenia period depended on game, and hunting was the major occupation. Prehistoric man's concern with animals is evidenced in the accurate representations found engraved in bone, antlers, pebbles, and walls. Prehistoric art is action art, alive and moving. (Musée des Antiquities, Saint Germain-en-Laye)

5-10

5-11

Figure 5-10. *Tiger Resting* by Eugene Delacroix, French, 1830. Although frequently critized for "his inability to draw correctly," Delacroix was one of the most expressive and most influential artists of his time. His drawings and paintings, such as this oil painting, express the energy, gesture, and power of the tiger with little attention to precision or "correct style." (Courtesy of the Art Institute of Chicago. Henry Field Memorial Collection)

Figure 5-11. With the power and the sureness of Picasso, this seven-year-old child has painted a cat that bristles, arches, and howls. With the fewest possible brush strokes, the young artist has expressed vividly her concept of a cat. (Courtesy of *Everyday Art Magazine*)

which captures a mood or impression, may call for rough-textured papers and thicker media such as tempera paints, chalks, or water colors.

The basic materials used for drawing and painting with children include flat bristle brushes of different sizes, which are often used in tempera paints. A round brush with softer bristles, commonly (but inaccurately) called a camel's hair brush, is used with water colors and with temperas. Both types of brushes are available in a range of qualities, and their useful lives depend a good deal upon the care they are given after each use.

Two basic water-soluble paints are water colors, which usually are packaged in metal boxes in a complete range of colors, and temperas, which may be packaged in liquid form, as dry powder, or as a cake. The type a teacher selects often depends on personal preference, for they are of essentially the same quality. Water colors are usually transparent when used for a thin color or wash on paper, whereas temperas generally are opaque.

Other colors come in the form of sticks, the most common of these being the wax crayon. Chalk, pastels, marking pens and pencils, and oil crayons are also common color materials that are used directly on dry surfaces.

There are unlimited types of surfaces on which to draw and paint, but they fall into only a half dozen categories: smooth or textured; absorbent (soft finished), or nonabsorbent, or (hard finished); light or dark; colored or uncolored; and large or small. There are, in addition, specialized surfaces such as canvas papers, canvas boards, colored tissues, and fiberboard. At the least the classroom will need standard white and manila drawing papers, newsprint and easel papers (for the younger children), colored construction and poster papers, and kraft wrapping paper.

THE BLACKBOARD

When the teacher wants to see boys and girls truly and intently occupied in a creative process, especially in the lower elementary grades, he can set aside one portion of the blackboard and each day permit a few youngsters to draw on it with colored chalk. Something about this experience intrigues the children. Perhaps it is the size of the blackboard or the brilliance of the chalk or the knowledge that what they make can easily be erased or changed (though it seldom is) that opens up new avenues and permits children the freest sort of self-expression.

This is an activity in which the materials themselves often seem to be stimulating enough to make the children want to draw. Some children whose work seems tight and tense in drawing lessons with common drawing or painting materials may quickly find themsleves while working on the blackboard. This is by no means a cure-all for children whose work is stereotyped. The good teacher

Figure 5-12. The blackboard can offer the freedom necessary for large, spontaneous drawings. For some children ideas come rapidly and must be recorded immediately. The blackboard is especially suited to group drawings. (Photograph by Ed Leos)

must constantly seek methods or materials that lend themselves to the children's individual differences, for no single material or method will ever be adequate to meet the needs of all the children.

Blackboard work presents certain small problems of cleanliness that need to be considered. Many older schools were not planned with small children in mind. Often one will find all the blackboards in a building at exactly the same height, which seems to have been determined by the teacher or the largest children, not the smaller ones. When this is the case, the young children have to reach up over the chalk troughs to work, and they frequently soil their sleeves. It is a good plan for the teacher to prepare, or have the mothers prepare, simple smocks for "dirty" activities. Most parents are eager to help, and when mothers are asked to make smocks from old shirts, they usually do so cheerfully. Collars can be removed, sleeves shortened, and elastic tape put in the ends of the sleeves to make the smock fit tightly at the wrists so that the sleeves may be pulled up above the elbows for such activities as finger painting. Smocks can be worn backward. Decorating the smocks can itself be an interesting project.

COLORED PAPER

A change of materials can be very stimulating. Occasionally the children should be given large pieces of colored paper and, if possible, be permitted to choose their own color. The older elementary and junior and senior high school boys and girls can achieve extremely beautiful results with colored chalks or pastels. Using large colored paper and soft chalks for outdoor sketching will result in brilliant and beautiful pictures. It is easy to obtain a good supply of drawing boards simply by having the children bring in large cardboard cartons and cut pieces from them about 18″ × 24″. These are light and much easier to handle and store than wooden drawing boards.

WET PAPER

If the chalk has a tendency to be dusty and occasionally soils desk tops and shirt-sleeves, the class might try an experiment working with colored chalks and wet paper. If a sink is available, the paper can be held together at the corners two sheets at a time, and submerged in the water. If this is done quickly, the sheets can be separated with the inside surfaces still dry and then placed on the desks with the wet side up. If a sink is not available, newspapers can be spread out on the desk tops and a small amount of water spread with a cellulose sponge until the whole surface of the drawing paper is wet. While the paper is wet, the child begins working with the chalk. The moisture holds the chalk dust and pulls a great deal of color from the stick, resulting in very brilliant pictures. This is an especially nice way of working when creating free and large designs.

If the class enjoys working with the wet paper, they may wish to try some other experiments with it. If dry powder paints and stiff brushes, such as easel brushes or brushes similar to those used for oil painting, are available, several children may experiment with this technique. Place a small amount of dry powder paint of each color in separate containers, such as jar lids or the compartments of muffin tins, and moisten a piece of heavy drawing paper or bogus paper (a gray porous drawing paper). Have the child dip the tip of a bristle brush into the powder paint; when he wipes it across the wet paper, the moisture on the paper will cause the powder to become liquid paint. On this stroke the brush will pick up enough moisture so that when it is dipped into a second color or back into the same color, it will pick up enough dry paint to make another stroke on the paper. Each time the brush touches the paper it picks up enough moisture to cause the dry powder to adhere. If the paper remains moist enough, the whole painting can be completed without the child's ever having to moisten the brush.

Rich and unusual effects can occur because of the paint fusion that takes place on the wet paper. Sometimes the paintings must dry and the children must rework certain areas to emphasize parts that blurred or became softer in color than they had wished. Correcting or overpainting is perfectly permissible if it helps the child to express himself more clearly. Processes that permit free expression of ideas are good processes. Teachers should help the children eliminate the fear of doing things the "wrong" way.

LARGE PAINTINGS

Teachers who work with very small children realize the importance of having large brushes and large materials for easel paintings because many small children like to fill spaces rapidly. Many types of excellent easel brushes are available to the classroom teacher, but sometimes he may wish to create his own oversized brushes by using ordinary paint or enamel brushes from the hardware store. These inexpensive, black-bristle brushes can be trimmed carefully so that their bristles are short and firm for easel painting. Another very good practice for large paintings is to cut a cellulose kitchen sponge into blocks about 1" square and 2" or 3" long. Several of these can supplement the brush supply, for the children can be taught to use them effectively for painting. The children can dip one end

Figure 5-13. After visiting a nearby chicken farm, the class uses the pleasantness of the outdoors for its classroom and the chickens for its subject matter. The drawing boards are large pieces of heavy cardboard called upson board. (Photograph by Ed Leos)

into the paint and quickly fill an entire sky or dress or tree without continually having to dip, as they must with a brush.

The classroom teacher should not be too disturbed by lack of easels or fancy art equipment. The floor is an excellent place to paint, in many respects better than an easel. Fine paintings can be made on brown wrapping paper, newspapers, drycleaning bags, and the sides of large cardboard cartons. Even if the class store-room is adequately stocked with conventional art materials, the teacher ought to try occasionally to bring variety into the program through the use of some of these other materials. An occasional use of unusual materials can stimulate child-ren to look and to conceive of old materials in new ways, and it can help do away with the idea that good art of creative work can be done only with expensive supplies.

FINGERPAINTING

Fingerpainting is an activity that is held in very high esteem in some quarters and looked upon as a very unpleasant activity in others. It lends a certain quality of freedom and release and at some time should be included in every arts and crafts program. However, many elementary school teachers omit fingerpainting for two main reasons. First, they believe that it is dirty, messy, and noisy and leads to confusion and chaos; second, they do not know or understand it.

Fingerpainting can be handled successfully by any teacher in almost any situation. Imagine the most primitive situation, in which the classroom is furnished with old-fashioned desks, each with its inkwell and a pencil trough, the desks screwed down to the floor in rigid rows, the tops slanting and too small. In such a room, the teacher must use the floor as the working space. Around the outer edge of the room he can have one of the children place a layer of clean newspapers, and on top of this the sheets of fingerpainting paper on which to work. The teacher can buy good fingerpaints from any school supply house, or make excellent ones in his own kitchen. To make fingerpaint, he would prepare a large portion

---

Figure 5-14. Painting of a rural scene by a teen-aged Egyptian youth. This painting is decorative and is almost like a large flat design. The student does not depend upon visual representation, as shown by the treatment of space, overlapping, and perspective. He paints the characteristics of each object rather than their visual appearance. The painting is highly successful in conveying what the child wishes to express and in its aesthetic appeal. (Courtesy of *Everyday Art Magazine*)

Figure 5-15. Watercolor painting by a Japanese teen-aged youth. Although this painting has a decorative quality similar to that in the Egyptian youth's painting, its treatment is completely different. Depending upon an understanding of visual space and perspective, the painting clearly describes the subject matter and has equal aesthetic appeal. (Courtesy of *Everyday Art Magazine*)

5-14

5-15

of ordinary starch. However, the proportion of starch to water is increased, so that the starch is considerably thicker than that used for laundry purposes. The novice might follow the following directions.

Mix dry starch with cold water until it is a smooth, thin paste; put it in the bottom of a large container and pour boiling water over it. If poured from a rather high position, the water goes down rapidly and churns up the starch paste, mixing it quickly and smoothly, so that no lumps result. If the water is added slowly, a dribble at a time, the starch is sure to become lumpy. Once the starch is mixed, the teacher can add a small handful of soap flakes or detergent. This will make it very easy for the children to clean their hands when they are through; or if paint should get into their clothing, the soap will make the paint easy to clean or wash out without leaving a stain. If a child should get some fingerpaint on his clothing, the teacher should see that it is allowed to dry; then it can generally be picked off with the fingernail without leaving any stain or mark. If the teacher tries to wipe the paint off while it is wet, the colors will only rub deeper into the fabric, making it more difficult to clean.

When the fingerpaint paper is in place, the children can kneel on the clean newspapers and the teacher can go around the room pouring a small panful of clear starch onto each child's paper. The teacher will quickly learn to judge the amount to pour on each paper. It is not necessary to moisten the papers because the starch contains enough moisture. One of the children can follow the teacher, sprinkling a small amount of powdered paint onto the clear starch. Now the children can begin to work, and the motions that they make on their paper will mix the paint and starch into a smooth color. This practice saves paint, because if any of the starch is left after painting, it can be stored for several weeks without spoiling.

The children should be encouraged to make large, free, rhythmic motions while painting, using closed fists, open hands, sides of the hands, lower arms, and knuckles. It is a good practice for them to make designs rather than pictures, because if they limit their activities to the rigid drawing of pictures, then the

Figure 5-16. Although fingerpainting was used as early as the eighth century by Chinese artists who smeared colors onto silk with their hands, in the Western world it is used mainly as a medium for children. It is a relaxing experience in which little concern is given to the finished painting. The painting itself is little more than a record of an unabashed feeling for rhythm. (Photograph by Ed Leos)

Figure 5-17. As thin tempera paint is brushed across a crayon drawing, the paint is resisted by the wax but absorbed into the paper on all areas not covered by the crayon. The picture thus changes its entire character. Children should be encouraged to experiment with such combinations of media. (Photograph by Ed Leos)

5-16

5-17

whole value of the process can be lost. With a starch mixture on the fingerpaint paper, the children are able to work for long periods of time changing their designs, wiping them out, and so on. If the paintings become a little sticky and the children wish to continue working, the teacher can simply add a bit more starch.

When the children feel that their paintings are complete, they should leave them on the floor, wash their hands, and return to their seats, ready for their next class. If no sink is available, a bucket of warm, soapy water, a scrubbing brush, and some large sheets of newspapers, in the absence of paper towels, on which to dry their hands should be placed somewhere near the center of the room to solve the clean-up problem. At the first recess, the teacher can have one of the children gather the dry paintings and another gather the newspapers that were beneath them. The old newspapers can be destroyed and the paintings displayed.

The fingerpaintings can be used for notebook covers or to decorate waste-baskets made of old five-gallon ice cream cartons. They can be pressed flat with a warm iron and will make interesting displays around the classroom wall. They always look more attractive if they can be matted or carefully mounted on a larger piece of paper. If fingerpaint paper is not available or is too expensive for the classroom budget, fingerpaintings can be done on almost any type of paper, but preferably one with a smooth, nonporous surface. Magazine covers, butcher paper, and shelf paper are all good for this activity. Shelf paper is perhaps the most satisfactory.

As was explained in the section on printmaking, the use of a sheet of smooth formica, safety glass, or an enamel-topped table is best for fingerpainting. Done directly on one of these nonporous surfaces, the painting can be duplicated with little effort if one places a sheet of newsprint or drawing paper on the moist painting, then gently rubs it with the hand. The painting is transferred from the formica to the paper without wrinkling. This saves buying expensive fingerpaint paper in large quantities, since almost any paper will be satisfactory. Most children thoroughly enjoy fingerpainting activities and will want to indulge in them often.

Occasionally the feel of fingerpaint may be repulsive to a child. When this is the case, the teacher is unwise to force the child to continue, but rather should permit him to engage in an activity that is more pleasant to him.

CRAYON RESIST DRAWING

Most classrooms are equipped with wax crayons, but often they are used only to make crayon drawings on manila or white paper. There are a number of good variations that the teacher might try with crayons to enrich and enliven his program. Occasionally when the children make crayon drawings, the teacher may have them work their drawings over very heavily, pressing the wax on as thickly as possible and leaving some areas entirely free of crayon.

When the drawings have been completed, the teacher may suggest that the children mix a small quantity of a dark water color and brush it over the entire surface of the drawing. The dark water color will fill in all areas that the crayon has not covered and will be resisted on those areas that the crayon has covered. This may give the feeling of a night picture and thus change the entire character of the drawing. A second drawing might be made in which the child definitely uses the theme of "nighttime," or "in the theatre," or "in the dark circus tent," or some similar theme allowing for major portions to be darkened and certain areas to be emphasized.

The child makes his drawing by planning what is going to happen when the water color or, in some cases, ink is washed across it. It is a thrilling experience to see the change that transpires when the water color crosses the paper, the sort of experience that enriches the program and causes the child to work and to imagine in ways previously unknown to him.

CRAYON SGRAFFITO

Another crayon process is sgraffito, which can be done in a manner similar to the resist. Each child is given a piece of smooth paper or oaktag, perhaps 9″ × 12″ or 10″ × 14″. With a bright color, he should begin to cover the surface of the paper, putting one color here and another there, occasionally blending two together, until the whole surface is entirely covered with bright colors. When this is done, the child selects his black crayon and puts a surface coating over the other colors. This can be done with India ink instead of waxed crayon. When the top has been entirely blackened, the child begins to make his picture by using some pointed tip or an old pen point to scratch through the top layer and expose the color beneath the surface.

This method intrigues children who are interested in minute detail and great accuracy. Some children are probably bothered by the fact that they cannot get rich detail when they are compelled to use large, blunt crayons for drawing. The teacher should be aware of the need for such a variety of experience so that each child can have an opportunity to find himself in one medium or another.

COLLAGE

The collage is a type of abstraction made with fragments of many types of materials pasted or fastened together into an artistic composition of contrasting textures.

Widespread use of such materials first appeared during World War I, when artists and teachers found themselves compelled to experiment with substitute materials because good art supplies were scarce. This forced improvization led to a new and interesting phase of experimental art, many fine examples of which are exhibited in our major galleries. The later work of Matisse, for example, shows the great effect of the collage upon contemporary art.

Teachers know that inexpensive and so-called waste materials and odds and ends like buttons, costume jewelry, ribbons, sequins, rickrack, fabric scraps, and so on are invaluable in the average classroom. To these are added the natural materials. All of these are best arranged in separate boxes, so that similar types are grouped together. The child quickly learns the special features and uses of individual materials, and he is able to develop a tactile sense, along with his visual sense, that helps him to distinguish between them. All first projects in collage generally result from simple, spontaneous ideas excited by the materials, and they may often turn into representational projects. The later collage experiments with older children can be guided, and many of the principles of design can be incorporated indirectly and emphasized as the need arises. Collage problems in mood or in opposites are good ones to work in. Urge the children to express their feelings through a sensitive selection of colors, sizes, and shapes, and by the placement of elements on the cardboard background. The problem of opposites will help make the children more sensitive to the different kinds of materials. A problem that encourage them to place large against small, light against dark, shiny against dull, rough against smooth, and thick against thin will help accomplish this purpose.

Collage projects are often carried to extremes; teachers may overuse them, or they may become an end in themselves, especially when all art becomes nonobjective "designs." Such projects sometimes become very popular because they offer rapid and spectacular results with minimal motivation. The teacher must be aware that the good program needs balance at all times, and whereas adventures

---

Figure 5-18. *Great White Whale, Moby Dick,* by Benton Spruance (1904–1967). This American artist used a variety of sources for his subject material, including religious, mythological, and fictional topics. This drawing, although simple in composition, is bursting with power and energy. (Courtesy of the National Gallery of Art, Washington, D.C.)

Figure 5-19. "Chicken" collage painting by an eight-year-old child. The practice of combining materials in a single work of art is not new. There are examples in many cultures from ancient times. In an effort to overcome the limitations of traditional materials, many artists have added unfamiliar materials to conventional media. This child has pasted her chicken to a background, added feathers, and painted a cage.

5-18

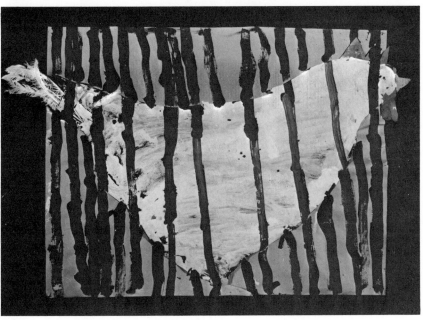

5-19

in materials are of utmost importance, they can only supplement the good drawing and painting program based upon the individual experiences of the children.

CRAYON ENCAUSTICS

The classroom teacher may find that he is accumulating many small, variously colored pieces of crayon. Crayon encaustic will help to dispose of them. The teacher may drop bits of each color into the six or eight depressions of an old muffin tin, keeping all the reds in one, all the blues in another, all the greens in a third, and so on. Melt these over a hotplate covered with a cookie sheet, which will prevent drippings from soiling the plate by falling into the coils and causing smoke or flame. While these crayons are in a liquid form, they can be used in the same way as oil paints. Stiff-bristle brushes are far superior to hair brushes for this process. The wax cools and dries very rapidly when it is removed from the muffin tin, so that children must learn to work very fast and with little attention to detail. Because of the speed with which they are made, the pictures are brilliant and fresh and display techniques not seen in any other medium. Because it requires a certain speed and dexterity, this is a project that works best in the junior and senior high schools.

After the paintings are covered, students can conduct experiments by adding additional heat to the painting with a small alcohol torch, thus causing further fusing of color. This type of painting can be done on practically any surface. Old posters or pieces of cardboard, scraps of masonite, and cardboard boxes are all good surfaces on which to work. Students can give the completed paintings done with this hot wax method additional interest by using some of the scratch methods described for the crayon sgraffito process, and then buffing.

WATER COLOR PAINTING

We often find boys and girls who have lost confidence in their ability to create. This loss of confidence generally occurs when there is a discrepancy between what the child can produce and what he wishes he could produce. In other words, his technical skills have not caught up to his mental maturity or his conscious awareness. When this occurs it is important for the arts and crafts teacher to find ways to help the child regain confidence in his creative ability and permit him to make drawings or painting or crafts that will satisfy his critical nature. This period of development generally occurs in the upper elementary or junior high school years, and sometimes in senior high school.

One method of restoring confidence is the accidental water color. The student is given a large piece of drawing paper, which he saturates with water. Then the teacher announces that the class will do water color experiments, trying to create moods with the colors. The first mood could be a happy one. The individual should decide which colors are "happy," then moisten each of these in his water color box. When all the chosen colors are wet, he should pick one up with his brush, put it on the paper in any way he wants, then move on to the next color, being careful never to cover one color with another. He should continue in this way until the entire paper is covered with colors that will fuse in very unusual ways and create all sorts of brilliant accidents.

While this paper is drying, the teacher may ask the students to think up another mood, perhaps an unpleasant one, and then to think of all the colors that seem appropriate. This time they may use dark colors, such as black, purple, dark gray, and browns, and again they will cover the entire surface with colors. In this exercise, the teacher may wish to have the paper even wetter than in the first, thus creating entirely different sorts of color fusions. If large puddles remain, these can easily be blotted with the tip of the brush or with an ink blotter. The teacher should exercise caution to see that the paintings are not picked up while they are still wet, causing all the colors to fuse into a kind of homogenized gray.

On the next lesson, the class may take the first painting—the light one—and the teacher may talk about it as though it were a sky that the students had seen early one bright, sunny morning while riding the bus to school. A discussion of other things seen that day may ensue, and the students can sketch these things on the surface of the bright water color sky. From this point on, black water color or India ink is used, and the opaque foreground contrasts with the brilliance of the background, giving a very dramatic effect. The second picture may be used to sketch things seen silhouetted against a night sky. These, too, can be painted with black water color or India ink. Other pictures can be made of skylines or shorelines, or even to create the illusion of a body of water.

The best subject matter is always derived from the experiences of the children, and teachers will realize that what has just been described is a very limited process. But when the class is filled with children who are unwilling or unable to create, the teacher must do something in order to start them working. This procedure does much to help them regain their confidence. No procedure will prove to be a panacea, nor will a few simple words whispered into the ear of a child change an attitude, but after several lessons of this sort the children are generally ready to try new things. Through such an experience, they may gain confidence in their teacher and in themselves. From this point on, teaching becomes a much more pleasant and rewarding experience.

If water colors are not available, the same method can be used with tempera paints, which are more opaque, but are very rich and lend themselves better to

5-20

5-21

overpainting. If both water colors and tempera paints are available, the teacher may begin with the transparent water colors on an opaque foreground and move on to tempera on wet paper. Then, instead of using black, the teacher may permit the children to use whatever colors they desire for the foreground. In this manner, the teacher can work toward freer, more expressive paintings.

PAINTING ON WINDOW GLASS

Most of the drawings that boys and girls make in the classroom end up mounted or matted and hung on the wall or bulletin board. Occasionally, for variety, the teacher may wish to make a stand-up picture. A square piece of window glass and a short length of 2" × 4" lumber that has been notched to hold the glass are all that is needed for a stand-up picture. Using any paints that will adhere to glass and have a transparent quality, the children can paint stand-up pictures to be placed in front of windows. The light passes through the pictures and creates the appearance of stained glass. Some excellent paints are available to the classroom teacher for this sort of activity. However, he can make an adequate substitute by adding a sufficient quantity of clear varnish to colored enamels, which will render the enamels translucent.

IN CONCLUSION

There are many other ways of painting in the classroom, and as in all phases of the art program, the classroom teacher must use the available materials and use them sometimes in nonstandard ways. It is important to be experimental, but it is not a good idea to turn one's back upon good standard practices. Some teachers feel that they should not use any method that has been tried before or used successfully by others. This is pure folly.

Often teachers ask, "What is the right way to use water colors? What is the

---

Figure 5-20. One of the most important parts of art education is the development of the critical abilities of children. Part of this development results from experiences in which children are encouraged to view and verbalize. Sensitive guidance through discussion and questions by the teacher results in free and open responses from the children.

Figure 5-21. Painting is one of the best outlets for a mind full of ideas needing direct, positive expression, for here they can be translated into tangible form in a matter of minutes. Complex ideas are presented with paint and crayons far earlier than with written or even spoken words. The interpretation of the environment through painting is one essential aspect of the creative development of the child. (Photograph by Donna J. Harris)

5-22

5-23

right way to use crayons?" The answer is that there is no right or wrong way so long as the children have the opportunity to express themselves in their own manner. Children are like great painters in that they develop their own techniques through working and not through listening.

Figure 5-22. *John Brown going to His Hanging,* Horace Pippin (1888–1946). Primitive painting in the United States began in the early part of the nineteenth century. Although untrained, most primitive painters work hard to develop their personal techniques and styles. Pippin painted mainly what he remembered with great accuracy, in detail, and with a natural sense of design. He knew or cared little about perspective or lights and shadows. His strength is found in the sincerity and honesty of his paintings. (Pennsylvania Academy of the Fine Arts, Philadelphia)

Figure 5-23. *Work in Field* by Ivan Vecenaj, Yugoslavia. This fine example of a primitive oil painting on glass illustrates how it is possible for a man without formal training, isolated from the mainstream of official or accepted art and using only his own resources and ingenuity, to create art. In Yugoslavia such art developed spontaneously in many rural villages and is considered peasant or folk art. (The Gallery of Primitive Art, Zagreb)

Figure 6-1. First-grade children made these tree ornaments from salt ceramic. They were molded into a variety of simple shapes and, while they were still pliable, a knotted string was pressed into them. After drying, they were painted with tempera paints. (Photograph by Ed Leos)

six

SEASONAL ACTIVITIES AND THE HOLIDAYS

Special occasions associated with national holidays and religious calendars have always been important in the history of crafts, not only for their traditional customs but for the opportunity for creating special new objects for each occasion. Costumes, masks, noisemakers, effigies, processional objects like banners and flags, special foods, toys, and many types of decorations have all been part of the craftsman's special contribution. Even today in our sophisticated society many of these same traditions still remain in the annual celebration of Halloween, Chanukah, Christmas, the Fourth of July, Thanksgiving, and other holidays. For the many ethnic groups within our larger culture there are a myriad of special holidays, each with its own traditions and customs. It is in the preservation and recognition of these subculture activities that much of the richness of our dominant culture is attained. Education ought to help children to understand and appreciate the meaning and the beauty of the traditions and customs of other cultures as well as our own.

Art work for special occasions can bring out the very best and the very worst in classes. Some of the richest experiences and deepest feelings that children have are experienced at holiday seasons or during special events. We know, for example, of the special feelings of most children during the Christmas season when stores, homes, and religious institutions, as well as the school and the classroom, are full to overflowing with the feeling and the beauty of the holiday. Instead of feeling that something novel is necessary, the teacher can turn to the so-called "standards," such as modeling, drawing, painting, stitchery, and so on, and use the strong motivation of the holiday as the basis for these activities. Making a crèche, a wall hanging, or a lovely painting are all fine special activities. Unfortunately, some schools do not make the most of these rich experiences, but rather use the holidays to pass out patterns and decorate the schools with the poorest kinds of stereotyped materials. Walls and windows are filled with row upon row of Santas, pumpkins, or snowmen, each exactly like the rest. Generally these patterns are almost devoid of the real meaning of the season. Some schools discourage or prohibit the teaching of religious subjects on school time, but many have no objection to an impartial examination of the holidays of all religions.

MURAL MAKING

The making of large group murals provides an excellent outlet for the feelings created at special seasons and holidays and develops within the children a spirit of cooperation and an understanding of the problems of their classmates. Imagine a classroom of fourth-grade children who want to make a large mural on brown wrapping paper for the impending Christmas and Chanukah seasons. Through group discussion, the class may select "our town during the December holidays" as a topic. The teacher may suggest, "Let us write on the board everything that we know about our town. How many parts are there to our town?" Back come the answers: the business section, industrial section, residential section, and so on. After the main headings have been written on the blackboard, the teacher may ask, "What kind of buildings would we find in each section?" Soon the board will be filled with the things that the children know about their community. Then the teacher may ask, "What makes our community different now from what it is like at any other season?" Some will suggest snow, colored lights, decorations, Christmas trees, people shopping, bundles, and so on. Finally, when all the facts have been written on the board, the teacher can suggest that they begin and asks each child to select one thing that he wants to make. After each child has made his choice and begun to work, the teacher can select two or three children to prepare a background with tempera paint, chalk, or colored paper. They can work directly on the brown wrapping paper, which by now has been fastened onto the wall.

It is not necessary, or even good, to have a preconceived idea of how this may turn out, for as the children begin to work on the background, the ideas will flow freely. They will be able to solve the problems adequately without much assistance from the teacher. Meanwhile, at their seats, the children will be working along, some rapidly, some more slowly, and when the first ones finish, the teacher can suggest, "What important things have we omitted?" or "Suppose you start making the people or the trees." There is always a multitude of small details that need to be filled in, and by holding some of these back, a good balance can be kept on the use of class time so that all the children are working all the time.

When everyone has completed his task, including the small details, the group can put the work aside to discuss the organization of the mural. Now the teacher may ask, "What shall we put in the center of our mural?" and as decisions are made, one by one the buildings are brought up by the children and pinned temporarily to the background. Most likely there will be too many objects for each to be seen in its entirety, so the class will discuss the problem of overlapping. There may be an imbalance or poor distribution that the children will want to correct when they see the mural parts assembled. Through these overlappings in cut paper, the children can begin to understand the meaning of overlapping in drawing and painting. During the discussion the children will see that they need more of this or more of that, and later some children can volunteer to make the needed parts. Finally, when the group concludes that it has developed the best possible arrangement with the added parts, the whole mural is pasted into place.

In the end the children will experience a great delight in what they have accomplished as a group and will feel the real meaning and value of group activity. Each child will realize that he could not have done by himself what the group has done together. The poorest student can identify with this mural, realize that it is part his, and get a deep sense of accomplishment.

This mural procedure is only one of dozens of possible approaches. The class may use the same method by drawing or painting individual pictures, cutting them out, and pasting them on a background, or by having each child paint a part directly on a large mural. It is incorrect to think that one method is better than another. The teacher must simply make the decision as to what method will be most effective in his room based on the students' age, materials and time available, and interest.

PEEP SHOWS

No matter what their age, children always have an air of excitement and enthusiasm when they are making peep shows. A shoe box is good for a peep show, and almost any shoe store will be glad to provide a sufficient number of boxes for the average class. Good peep shows require some imagination in the selection of scrap materials and a solid motivation, so that they will not be trite or stereotyped. Common materials can easily be gathered—weeds, twigs, sawdust from the school shop, pebbles, stones, leaves, vines, cotton, sticks, and so forth.

At one end of the box, children cut a hole about the size of a quarter or fifty-cent piece with a pair of scissors, and open the top at the opposite end to permit light to enter. Sometimes holes are also placed on the sides to give a kind of spotlight or theater lighting effect. The scene is built on the inside bottom of the box. For example, perhaps it will be an ice skating scene remembered from a winter vacation experience.

The children will easily think of uses for the scrap material available. A bit of broken mirror becomes an icy pond, broken twigs a campfire, crumpled cellophane the fire itself, colored papers the mountains in the background, bits of cotton hung on thread the clouds floating overhead, and a twig stuck in a piece of modeling clay a tree. Little figures may be modeled from plasticene or pipe cleaners. Here a stone may be a boulder and a bit of sand a mountain trail, and so it goes, with children finding new and imaginative uses for otherwise useless mater-

6-2

6-3

ials. This is the creative process. Finally, with colored cellophane covering some of the openings in the box, the child can light his peep show just as a stage designer lights his set, enlarging or closing one of the holes, changing from a piece of yellow cellophane to one of another color, thinking, deciding. In this constant flow of problems and solutions, of ideas and thoughts, is found the value of crafts in elementary education. For the child, the great thrill comes when he gets to peep into the opening of his neighbor's show and allows his to be viewed by others.

DIORAMAS

A peep show may be used in a large box with slight modifications if an entire side of the box is opened or if the lid of the box is not used and the box stands on its side. When the scene is constructed, the opening can be covered with a piece of cellophane, which provides a barrier between the viewer and the scene and gives the feeling of looking into another world. This diorama makes a fine group project in the same way that a cut paper mural does. In the study of a unit on a country, the festivals, holidays, national customs for example, the children may wish to construct a diorama as a culmination of all they have thought and learned from research and discussion during the study of the unit. Perhaps this time they can model larger figures, using the salt ceramic formula given in Chapter Two. Such activities enrich any learning situation and give the children a deeper feeling of identification with the things they study and make for a happier, more useful learning environment.

COOKIE DECORATION

Many special occasions call for small parties or treats at school, for which the teacher can have the children or their parents bring in plain, undecorated cookies. The children can have an interesting art lesson decorating the cookies for the party. All that is needed are some clean paper cups, a box of confectioner's sugar, a small quantity of milk, and some vegetable dyes. It is a good idea to mix one large cup

---

Figure 6-2. When children work together, they learn to value the ideas of others and to accept and respect the differences among people. The major lesson of cooperation is learned when the individual recognizes that what the group can accomplish almost always exceeds what he could accomplished by himself. (Photograph by Ed Leos)

Figure 6-3. The diorama is an excellent group project which teaches the values of cooperation and planning. This circus was constructed in a large cardboard container by about ten children. (Photograph by Ed Leos)

of powdered sugar with sufficient milk to attain the consistency of icing. The teacher can do this in a cup or bowl and then place some of the mixture in each of the paper cups. Several drops of vegetable dye can be added, and the mixture stirred with a spoon or tongue depressor. The children may then paint their designs on the cookies with the icing, using toothpicks or paste sticks as the painting instrument. There is no need to tell the children how to decorate a cookie, for they will come forth with highly imaginative and beautiful designs. The occasion should suggest the types of designs that the children create.

PAPER DECORATIONS

On some occasions, the children may desire to decorate the classroom for a party or a fair, or at Christmas, to decorate a tree. Every teacher knows that there are limitless possibilities for creating interesting and original decorations. Paper is the most effective and most readily available material for simple decorations. With scissors, and flat paper of various kinds, great varieties of interesting items can be made. The smallest child will cut uncomplicated forms directly from flat pieces of colored paper. When pasted upon a contrasting colored paper, these make effective wall decorations. They can also be hung separately from threads for gay and colorful decorations.

Many surprises await the child when first he folds a sheet and cuts through

Figure 6-4. Christmas Bread of Unleavened Dough, Czechoslovakia. Bread and pastry doughs are adaptable to many forms and can be modeled much like clay or pressed into molds that are already shaped. Since antiquity, especially in the Hellenistic-Roman period, the preparation of food has been sometimes treated as an art that included visual beauty as well as good taste. (Schweizerisches Museum für Volkskunde, Basel)

Figure 6-5. Boards like this one from Switzerland were carefully carved in intaglio, most often in groups of a dozen or more squares to mark the lines between cookies. The finished cookies were made of thin dough pressed into the mold, removed, and baked. They were sometimes kept for months and often became so hard that it was said that it was as easy to eat the board as the cake. (Courtesy of the Musée de l'Homme, Paris)

Figure 6-6. *Robot,* Mary Benson Stickney. This simple gingerbread figure is an example of edible art. In addition, there are fortune cakes, wedding cakes, fertility breads, and Easter and Christmas specialties. (Museum of Contemporary Crafts of the American Craftsmen's Council)

Figure 6-7. Art first entered the kitchen in the form of cookie cutters, butter molds, and cookie and cake molds. Carved honeycake, gingerbread, and springerle molds are still used to make decorative foods for special occasions. Hardwood boards are carefully carved in relief. Dough is rolled thin, laid on the board, carefully pressed into the carved area, and then lifted off. The dough rises very little when it bakes, so the designs remain clear and sharp. (Courtesy of the Tiroler Volkskunstmuseum, Innsbruck)

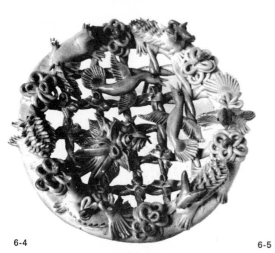

6-4

6-5

6-6

6-7

6-8

6-9

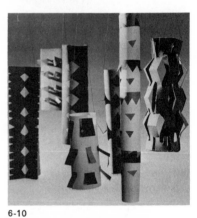

6-10

Figure 6-8. The Polish decorate many of their homes with elaborately patterned cutouts of colored paper, which they paste to the walls or mount and hang from the ceilings. The Swiss also did much work in cut paper, including the use of the silhouette and appliqués of colored paper. (Courtesy Musée de l'Homme, Paris)

Figure 6-9. This hanging ornament of cut and twisted paper is traditional Polish. Festivals, carnivals, and holidays are prominent in folk cultures, not only for their tradition, but as an occasion to decorate and make costumes, masks, toys, and special foods. (Museum of Contemporary Crafts of the American Craftsmen's Council)

Figure 6-10. Special occasions call for decorations to add a bit of gaiety to the classroom. These are constructed of colored paper that has been folded and cut with scissors or rolled into tubes and decorated with pieces of different-colored paper. They hang by threads from light fixtures. (Photograph by Ed Leos)

two thicknesses at once, thus duplicating his design. He follows this by making increasingly complex folds, or by making single folds with more intricate cutting. These processes are, in a sense, learned by being done. The child will soon wish to appliqué additional colors and shapes. Sometimes the forms and added pieces are bent, folded, or twisted to give a three-dimensional quality to the cut paper, thus becoming a form of paper sculpture. Whole pictures can be made in this way. When the paper work begins to move into three dimensions, it is wise to have such aids as clear tape, staplers, and rubber cement available to make the work more effective.

Children may make beautiful decorative forms of plain paper strips bent into circles, loops, spherical combinations, and so forth. They may wrap flat sheets to become cylinders or cones, sometimes decorating the surfaces with added pieces or with open designs that have been cut away from the flat sheet. Often small shapes can be folded and then cut, pasted to additional similar shapes, or decorated with added bits to be strung with needle and thread as hanging decorations.

As the children progress in their paper problems, they will discover ways to cut paper to make it expand as it hangs, or to have volume as it stands. The old "Japanese lantern" that most teachers made in school years ago was a combination of several of these processes, but it was invariably approached so unsubtly that the children had no chance for creative interpretation. Many patterns are available for making decorations, but they are meaningless to the child because he has had no part in designing them. Even though it may sometimes be difficult to do, teachers and parents should constantly think of the activities of the classroom in terms of their value to the children. The child should never be secondary to the product he makes. This is not to imply, however, that the product is of no value or importance, for the product is always a record of the child's experience. If it is a deep experience and the child is sufficiently motivated, the product will invariably be good when measured by developmental standards rather than by adult standards. If the experience is shallow or meaningless, the child will not care and the product will have little meaning for him.

EGG SHELLS

Eggs are used in almost every household and are therefore generally available for craft work. The trick is to use the eggs without breaking the shells, which one can do by penetrating each end of the egg with a small hole and blowing out the contents for scrambled eggs. There are always enough interested parents who will try to save hollow egg shells for classroom activities. In some instances, hardboiled eggs will serve just as well. The eggs can be decorated with water colors, tempera paints, wax crayons, or with glue and glitter, cut paper, or metallic paper pasted on. When hung by a thread, these make attractive Christmas balls.

Another project with eggs (these can be hard boiled), is to make miniature ladies' heads wearing Easter hats. A simple collar can be made of a strip of construction paper large enough to hold the egg so that it sits solidly. Children can develop faces with paints or colored papers, colored pencils, or colored scrap materials. Finally, each child can design an Easter hat to sit on top of the head. By this time the children will also be thinking of ways to make hair, scarves, bows, and so on. This can also serve as an interesting fashion project. Actually, the eggs can be used for a multitude of small figures, for the egg shape may suggest birds, fish, animals, insects, rocket ships, in fact, anything that is in any way oval. While the child works with the egg, he should also consider the many possibilities of the egg carton and how the interesting pressed shapes of the paper dividers lend themselves to a variety of uses.

SALT CERAMIC AGAIN

The salt and cornstarch mixture described in Chapter Two lends itself well to making tree ornaments or decorations. Among the simplest forms will be little balls that the children can roll in the palms of their hands and into which they can pinch a bit of string that will dry in place and can be used for hanging. When dry, these balls can be decorated with paints or glitter. Smaller balls may have a matchstick pushed through the center of them to form beads of all sizes, shapes, and descriptions; when painted and strung, these make beautiful hangings for the elementary school Christmas tree. Sometimes the salt ceramic can be pressed out flat like pie dough, and with a dull paring knife the children can cut out shapes in the same way they would cut out Christmas cookies. Once again, a bit of string stuck into them while wet will serve to hang them. When dry, these can be painted on both sides and decorated as the children desire. Small figures, birds, butterflies, insects, and geometric shapes would be interesting to make from the salt ceramic. A little soft wire stuck into the bottom of a bird before it dries could be used to wrap it around a tree branch; a short length of string stuck in its back before it dries would help it to fly when hung overhead in the room.

Although modeling and sculpting were discussed fully in Chapter Two, it might be suggested at this point that the salt ceramic lends itself excellently to the making of crèches, Santa's reindeer, carolers, and other modeled figures. Most of these projects could also be made from the papier-mâché pulp described in Chapter Eight.

6-12

6-11

6-13

Figure 6-11. Gingerbread. Edible art takes many forms—the wedding cake, fortune cookies, fertility breads, holiday cookies. This fine gingerbread was made by first gently pressing stiff dough into a mold carved of wood, removing the dough, and baking it. (Courtesy Musée de l'Homme, Paris)

Figure 6-12. *Des Oeufs Pour La Fete* by M. Avati, Italian School. The egg, a universal fertility symbol, became part of art as people began decorating them for the celebration of Christian Easter. Designs are made with wax and dye, painting, and appliqué of cloth, paper, and glitter. This mezzotint print uses the painting of eggs as its subject matter. (The National Gallery of Art, Washington D.C. Rosenwald Collection)

Figure 6-13. Children in elementary school decorated these eggshells with paints, papers, and glitter. They are hung by threads in a tree branch brought into the classroom for that purpose.

GLASS

Elementary teachers might shudder at the very notion of bringing glass into the classroom. However, types of glass are available that add great glamor to a Christmas tree. A visit to a local hardware store or lumberyard will provide bits of glass in a variety of widths and lengths for decorating with colored enamels or with commercial art paints, which are available for use on glass and nonporous surfaces. If the teacher exercises care and caution and instructs his pupils adequately on the handling of the glass, there should be no difficulty. These bits of glass can be painted and decorated and then allowed to dry. Hangers are made from small pieces of brown gummed tape and the pieces hung here and there on a Christmas tree by means of thin nylon or silk threads that are long enough to allow some swinging movement of the pieces. These will sparkle and shine and add beauty and life to the tree. Some of these pieces will be large enough to be used for stand-up paintings, such as those described in Chapter Five.

BANNERS AND FLAGS

The banner is a device used universally for creating atmosphere for parades, celebrations, or special days. It is sometimes used in religious rites and ceremonies. One seldom sees banners and flags being used as an art form in the elementary classroom, and yet this project is one of the most satisfying and enjoyable that the children can do. With the very smallest children, a class period devoted to making marching flags is most rewarding. Using thin strips of wood acquired from the scrap boxes of the school shop or the local lumberyards and rectangles of brown wrapping paper, each child can design his own flag, using paints or crayons, colored papers, or the materials that are normally found in scrap boxes in the classroom. However, on certain seasonal or holiday occasions, the entire room can be decked in flags and banners representing the occasion. Here its real meaning can be stressed and each child can express in his own way the meaning of that particular holiday or season in a long flowing banner made of brown wrap-

Figure 6-14. *Tablet Commemorating a Victory of King Narmer,* 1st Dynasty, Egypt. This ancient votive pallette of slate shows the triumphant king with his courtly retinue and two Mesopotamian monsters. Shown in the detail, top right, are the slaves marching before the Pharaoh carrying emblematic standards. These processional standards were the forerunners for banners and flags. (Courtesy of Egyptian Museum, Cairo)

Figure 6-15. For this parade, banners were made of brown wrapping paper stapled to strips of soft wood. Each child has designed his banner according to his interpretation of the 4th of July. This type of activity helps break the stereotypes that so often are part of holiday art. (Photograph by Ed Leos)

6-14a

6-14b

6-15

ping paper or shelving paper or ordinary white paper. The child can attach one end of the banner to a strip of wood with staples or glue, and can hang the banner from the classroom ceiling or from a wire stretched from wall to wall. The child can also make banners and flags on fabrics and add the decorative elements by sewing other fabrics on to the surface of the large piece.

CLASSROOM WINDOWS

Using the classroom windows is a good idea, but not to display stereotypes or to copy windows of great churches. Instead, the teacher should allow the children to invent original uses for this space. There are excellent paints available now that go on glass very easily and are easily washed away. These would do to make large paintings on the windows. Windows may also be covered with thin white tissue paper, tracing paper, or acetate, and children can make beautiful designs or pictures by applying transparent cellophane or paint to these areas. Occasionally, if the windows consist of small panes, each child may be assigned a single pane to plan a design for. He may use black construction paper with areas cut out and bits of transparent paper and cellophane inserted in the open areas as a solution to the problem. Here again the teacher knows the limits of the situation. Some schools may permit only the application of designs made of cut paper and paste applied by means of clear tape, whereas others may encourage the use of the windows for painting and decoration. When this is the case, the teacher should use every opportunity to display the children's work.

IN CONCLUSION

The types of activities that one can engage in during special seasons and holidays are limitless. Using many of the procedures described in this book we can make adaptations of valentines, and almost any occasion might call for a card, a placemat, or a special type of decoration. A discussion with the boys and girls in the class can solve many of the teacher's problems. A simple question, "What do you think we could do for Thanksgiving (or Veterans' Day or Washington's Birthday)?" will bring forth a large variety of responses from the children, especially if the teacher creates a good climate for free and original thinking. Each special occasion ought to challenge us in such a way that our programs become richer each year and our projects more personal, more individual, more meaningful each time they are tried.

6-17

6-16

Figure 6-16. This decorative object was made by inserting whittled quills into a round ball of wax. Although this style of ornament is popular today as a seasonal ornament, it was used as a votive offering in generations past. This particular object was prepared and hung in a religious shrine for a woman who was ill. (The Bayerisches Nationalmuseum, Munich)

Figure 6-17. In primitive and popular cultures, often called folk cultures, aesthetic and creative efforts usually are devoted to products for everyday use. Yugoslavs did straw work in braided and woven objects. (Courtesy of Musée de l'Homme, Paris)

Figure 7-1. Much of our knowledge of the domestic lives of the early Greeks is derived from small terra cotta figures such as this. Dating from the fifth century B.C., it represents a woman teaching a child how to cook. Other examples show men fixing fires, people using cooking utensils and bake ovens, and kitchens filled with various kinds of pots and pans. (Reproduced courtesy of the Museum of Fine Arts, Boston)

seven

CERAMICS

Ceramics is a term that generally covers any activity in which objects are formed of clay and hardened by heat. Because the raw material, clay, exists in all parts of the world, it has been a medium of expression and utility throughout the history of civilization. To trace the history of ceramics is to trace the history of man. For thousands of years, clay has been fashioned into containers, sculptures, toys, bricks, and tiles. Clay was first used primarily for containers to store food; later it was used for modeling and still later for building.

Pottery making first appeared among the ancient food gathering and agricultural peoples of Europe, Asia, and the Mediterranean area during the beginning of the neolithic culture, as early as the seventh or sixth millenia B. C. The oldest examples of ceramics were crudely fashioned containers of sun-dried pottery formed of pure clay. Later examples were made of clay and chopped grass and were fired, or heated, by some simple method.

Clay, which is dug from the surface of the earth, has been used in many different degrees of purity, from the very coarse which is full of minerals, organic materials and carbon, to the highly refined state, from which all foreign materials have been removed. The presence of various foreign materials accounts for much of the variation in appearance in ceramics, as do the many different colors and textures in clay.

Methods of pottery making that have existed for thousands of years are still fundamental to today's ceramist, or potter. They include the free-hand method of pinching a pot from a simple lump of clay with the thumb and fingers and the construction of containers by joining coils of clay or slabs of clay. Another simple method is the forming of a clay object over another form to give it shape, removing it once the shape is obtained, then allowing it to dry. Other methods include pouring liquid clay into a porous mold so that the clay adheres to the walls of the mold and takes the shape of the mold. A primary method used by many potters is wheel throwing, a method of shaping pottery from a lump of moist clay rotating on a wheel.

The forms of clay, the refinements of the processes, and the uses of clay are so numerous that one can know about only a few of them. Clay is not just a product of the past, but one of the most widely used materials for useful objects.

Clay is gathered in various ways. Sometimes it is mined in the form of a dry, almost rocklike material, which is crushed, ground, and refined before water is added to make it plastic. Often it can be discovered along the banks of streams, where children with shovels can easily remove it. One contemporary potter crawls deep into a small cave where he finds clay, refined by thousands of years of gently dripping water, in almost perfect condition for wheel throwing.

Moist clay is a plastic material that yields to the desires of the artist. It can be shaped, reshaped, then reshaped again. It can dry into a hardened but fragile shape, then crushed and powdered and later restored to plastic form by the addition of water. This can be done over and over until the piece is fired, at which time the clay changes and is never again water soluble.

This chapter will cover only a few processes, ones that have direct application to work with children. Specific details on glazes, firing, and clay bodies can be found elsewhere.

PREPARING CLAY

The most convenient form of clay is the ready-mixed moist clay that is available from many commercial sources. Since the advent of the air-tight plastic bag liners, this clay comes in good condition and can be easily kept. Because of the weight of the water in the clay, however, shipping costs make it far more expensive than dry, powdered clay. (An easy method of mixing dry clay—the plastic bag method—was discussed in Chapter Two.) If a very large quantity of clay is needed, a crock, such as an old-fashioned pickle crock, a plastic bucket, or a small, galvanized garbage can, will serve well. Too large a container should be avoided because of the weight it will have when full of moist clay and the difficulty in reaching the bottom. As a rule of thumb, about three to four quarts of water are used with twenty-five pounds of clay.

Cover the bottom of the container with 1″ or 2″ of water, then sift dry clay through the fingers until the surface of the water is covered. Stir with a strong stick until the clay is completely mixed. If it is quite moist, add more dry clay and stir again. Repeat the entire process. If the clay is mixed in quantities such as described here, the mixing is not so exhausting. If in the end the clay is exceptionally moist, dust additional dry clay through it. The dry clay will absorb the excess moisture. Let the clay stand uncovered for a few days, checking it regularly for proper consistency. After several days, a portion of the clay can be removed from the container to see if it is the right consistency for working. When it seems to be a good consistency, cover it to prevent further drying.

Before working with the clay, the teacher should make several plaster bats

7-2

7-3

7-4   7-5

Figure 7-2. One of the earliest ways of decorating pottery was the rough application of small impressions on the outer surface of the object. This pot, several millennia old, was decorated by pressing a round shape into the soft, unbaked clay. This round-bottomed container also has a "combed" decoration alternating with the pressed one. (Reproduced courtesy of Kansallimused, Helsinki)

Figure 7-3. One of the most common means of decorating the surface of ceramic objects is with colored engobes or slips. The chipped portion of this ancient ceramic bird clearly shows the thickness of the engobe, which was probably applied by brushing. (Milwaukee Public Museum)

Figure 7-4. This complex group of stylized figures in an enclosure serves as a record of a religious ceremony of the Bronze Age (2400 B.C.). Such examples of ancient pottery tell of events in the same way that today's photographs do. They allow us to a great degree to reconstruct the cultures of the past. (Reproduced courtesy of the Cyprus Museum, Nicosia)

Figure 7-5. The midsection of this twelve-gallon nineteenth century American clay water cooler is decorated with cobalt blue figures in a landscape painted in a free brush style. It is an interesting combination of utility and decoration. (The Smithsonian Institution)

7-6

7-7

by mixing gauging plaster with water and pouring it into old pie tins. The solid plaster form is removed from the tins and dried. The porous dried plaster acts like a blotter in removing excess moisture from clay. For most of the projects described here, the clay can be used as it comes from the storage container. Working on the reverse side of a piece of oilcloth that is slightly damp, the children can knead their clay balls into a uniformly smooth mass. If the clay is too moist, they can either work it on a dry plaster bat until the excess moisture is absorbed, or dust a thin coat of dry clay onto the oilcloth and pick it up with the clay in the kneading process. If it is too dry, they can put a small amount of water on the hands. A little practice with clay will quickly reveal the answers to these problems. It is possible that one period can be devoted to having each child get his clay in good condition so that during the following period he can focus attention on the use of the clay. Each child's clay can be stored in small plastic freezer bags.

THE HAND, PINCH, OR THUMB POT

Probably the oldest and most natural way to make a ceramic pot is to roll a small quantity of clay into a ball with the hands. When the ball is round, the thumbs are slowly forced into the clay. The child slowly enlarges this initial depression and shapes it by gently pinching the clay. As it is pinched, the clay is rotated so that the walls that are forming have an even thickness and a uniform slope. Round and round the pot turns, becoming smoother and better shaped with each rotation. Finally, the pot is finished, although perhaps the child will want to alter the original round shape or ornament the surface of the edge with the impression from a stick, nail, button, or what have you. More important than ornamenting, however, is keeping the form simple and honest. Try not to have these fine little pots perverted to become "ashtrays for daddy."

Figure 7-6. Wherever clay exists, man has sooner or later found the means to use it. The use of the potter's wheel and the firing of clay have been discovered independently by cultures thousands of miles and many years apart. Here, as his wheel turns, a primitive Indian potter develops a bowl from a lump of clay, keeping one hand inside and one outside to control the shape and thickness of the wall. (Reproduced courtesy of Monkmeyer Press Photo Service, New York. Photograph by Fujihira)

Figure 7-7. The contemporary potter uses a potter's wheel built on exactly the same principles as those of centuries ago. Since he no longer is required to make hundreds of utilitarian objects for household use, his attention has turned largely to aesthetics. As a result ceramics has become one of the most expressive of contemporary crafts. (Photograph by Bill Coleman)

7-8

7-9

MODELED FORMS

The first modeled forms are closely related to the pinched pot. Beginning with a solid mass or ball of clay, the child gently pinches, pulls, or nudges the mass to create his image of an animal or figure. This method calls for the entire figure to evolve from the initial mass, without the addition of other pieces of clay. If this idea can be impressed upon the children, the ensuing pieces will be simple. Small details are usually eliminated, and the pieces will be likely to withstand drying and firing without damage. This is a difficult method for some children to grasp, as it is more natural for many children to want to construct their figures piece by piece, continually adding more clay. In time, both methods should be introduced and combined.

After the first hand modeling from a solid piece, the children will want to explore the possibilities of more complex and more greatly detailed figures. The larger the mass, the more likelihood of damage in the firing process, because of the air bubbles that are sometimes trapped and of moisture that may remain in the center of a thick mass. The following method may help eliminate these problems.

Have each child pat out a piece of clay until it is less than 1/2" thick. Each rolls a piece of paper toweling or newspaper into a round or oval ball. He then wraps the clay pat gently around the paper, forming a round or oval core to make a lighter-weight piece. He makes a hole in this ball, as there must be a place for the air to escape during the firing process, when the paper will burn up. Then they make additional parts. If it is to be an animal, the ball can serve as the body. Legs, tail, neck, and head are added a piece at a time. If the added pieces are fairly large, the paper core method can be used with them to reduce weight and drying time.

As he adds each piece, the child must prepare carefully the surfaces to be joined. First they should scratch the surfaces to roughen them; then they apply a thick paste of clay and water, called *slip*, to one or the other surface, and press the surfaces firmly together. Then he uses his fingertips to smooth away any traces of the joining. This process is repeated until the form is completely joined. The child will

Figure 7-8. The flexibility of clay and the many ways it can be used help the child to learn the concept of three-dimensional space and to form concepts of physical proportion. This child is placing a group of small figures he has constructed in an arrangement remarkably similar to the Bronze Age group shown earlier in this chapter. (Photograph by Bill Coleman)

Figure 7-9. The child learns to model by modeling, to paint by painting, to pound by pounding, and to create by creating. There are no shortcuts or substitutes for the basic learning that is essential to the fullest development of all children. (Photograph by Donna J. Harris)

soon learn that spindly legs cannot support a heavy body and that the clay dictates, to a large degree, what can be done with it. The joined figure can be detailed with additional modeling or with surface treatments, as the child sees fit. While still damp, it can be further enhanced by decoration with colored clays, called *engobes*, which are in a liquid form. The figure is then stored before firing until it is completely dry.

COIL POTS

The method used to create the coil pot is closely allied to the method of the joined modeled form. Working on the reverse side of a piece of oilcloth, the child makes a base for the pot either by patting a small piece of clay into the shape of a small cookie or by rolling out a uniform coil of clay with the palms of the hands and wrapping it around and around until a base is formed. He must rub the coils across with his fingers, dragging clay from one to another until he obtains a smooth, flat surface. Now he rolls additional coils, each about half an inch thick. Each coil should be long enough to encircle the base. The surface of the edge of the base is scratched, or *scored*. Slip is placed on the scoring and a coil put in place. The child rubs the base and the coil gently with a fingertip, causing clay to be dragged from one to the other and creating an interlocking bind. When the outside is rubbed, one of the fingers of the other hand should be supporting the inside of the pot opposite the spot where the rubbing is taking place. Slowly, as each coil is added, the pot rises. When the child wishes to change the shape of the pot, he adds shorter coils to bring the form in or longer ones to make it flare out. The child finishes the pot by rubbing it with his fingertips, texturing the surface, or by decorating it with engobes. He then puts it away to dry thoroughly.

Figure 7-10. The first modelings of children are simple and direct, free of everything extraneous. The things that are important to the child are included if only in the most simplified form. Here, one child rests on a brickwall in the schoolyard after strenuous play while the other does a headstand. Careful examination of these figures reveal simple details like eyeglasses, lips, fingers, a T-shirt, bricks for the wall, and so forth, for the sitting figure; facial details that have been incised, long hair, a suggestion of skirt, and so forth, on the headstand figure. The details, even at this early age, are completely different and the techniques of making the details are highly personal. One child put in the details with the point of a pencil as though she were drawing, whereas the other built up the details from additional pieces of clay.

Figure 7-11. One builds a coil pot by adding one complete coil at a time. Each coil is joined to the pot by brushing thin clay at the point of contact and scoring the surfaces to be joined with a sharp stick or the point of a pencil. The potter unites the coil and the pot by transferring clay from one to the other with the fingertips. Indian potters are so adept at this that their coil pots have all the grace and refinement of thrown pots.

7-10

7-11

The earliest coil pots, like the earliest pinch pots, should be kept simple and direct. Some children always want to duplicate cheap pottery they have seen. To counteract this, the teacher should try to bring in some good examples of simple forms.

THE SLAB METHOD

Again using the reverse side of an oilcloth, the child rolls the clay into slabs in the same way that pie dough is rolled. He uses two strips of wood about 3/8″ thick as guides to obtain uniform thickness, and a wooden rolling pin to flatten the clay. Using paper patterns, he cuts pieces from the flattened slabs. A paring knife is used for the cutting. The child assembles the base and walls one at a time, using the method of scoring and adding slip. The shapes of slab pieces are as numerous as the imagination can suggest.

TILES

A tile can be made in the same way as a slab. Using the sticks to assure uniformity, a large slab is made and then cut into pieces, one for each child. Using modeling tools made of ice cream sticks, tongue depressors, bobby pins, dowel rods, or any other improvised equipment, the children carefully carve the surfaces of the squares of clay to create their own tiles. The possibility of combining the works of a whole group should not be overlooked in planning this lesson. As always, it goes without saying that the teacher does more than merely furnish the materials and explain or demonstrate procedures. He stimulates the imagination of each child so that the child has something to draw on his tile.

Another way to make tiles is to coat each of the squares of rolled clay with a thick, uniform coating of colored engobe, which can be brushed directly onto the surface with a soft, flat brush. When it has become firm, but not dry, the child cuts through the layer of engobe with a nail or small V-gouge, like those used in linoleum cutting. This exposes the clay below, which, when fired, is a different color from the engobe. These tiles are simple, direct, and especially childlike in

Figure 7-12. Tiles made of this slabs of clay can be decorated and given unusual textures through the use of everyday objects. Here, for example, interesting designs have been made by using wooden forks, a gear, and the threads of a screw.

Figure 7-13. Ceramic bird feeder by Karen Karnes. Using clay in a very direct and uncomplicated way, this artist achieves forms which become part of the environment and not an intrusion into it. (The Museum of Contemporary Crafts of the American Craftsmen's Council)

7-12

7-13

7-14

7-15

their charm. Instead of coating the entire surface, the children can also use the engobes like tempera paint, painting directly on the surface of the tile.

Still another method of working with tile uses commercially made tiles, such as white bathroom tiles. These are decorated or painted with another commercial product called *overglaze*. This method is a great deal like painting with water colors, in both procedure and effect. Although it detaches the child almost completely from the earthiness of clay, this method nevertheless provides an interesting painting experience and is a way to preserve permanently the creative ideas of children. These tiles can be attached to the wall of the school library, cafeteria, or nurse's room after they have been fired.

PRESS MOLDS

The press mold process is very similar to the process used in making fancy cookies from wood press molds. First, a plaster mold, or matrix, is made in one of several ways. The simplest way it to pour wet plaster into small gift boxes to the thickness of about 1″. When the plaster has set up, but not dried completely, the box is peeled away. The child then carves the surface of the plaster using the point of a nail file, a linoleum gouge, or any other improvised tool. As in the plaster relief process described in Chapter Two, the deep cuts become the high spots on the finished piece, and the shallow cuts the low spots. Care should be taken to keep the cuts simple and smooth. When the plaster is dry, the children can roll the clay into slabs, cut it into appropriate sizes, and press it firmly into the carved impression. The clay will easily take on the shape of the carved area, and when withdrawn, it will have a precise mirror impression of the carving. If any lettering is to be part of the design, it is important to remember that it will be a mirror impression. The pressed piece can be trimmed and set aside to dry.

The sizes and shapes of the pressed pieces will be determined by their proposed use. They can be used as tiles, jewelry, tree ornaments, or just decorative pieces. It is usually better to use a white or near-white clay for these pieces, so that bright,

Figure 7-14. Seventeenth-century Dutch tiles. Using animals as their decorative motives, these Dutch tiles illustrate the extent to which detail and control are possible in decorating ceramics. Each tile is like a small painting. (The Metropolitan Museum of Art, Gift of W. R. Valentiner, 1908)

Figure 7-15. Seventeenth-century Mexican tiles: The Mexican craftsman cared less about detail in his tiles than about the use of bright, gay and colorful designs to achieve his effects. (Courtesy of the Art Institute of Chicago)

low-fire glazes can be used on them most effectively. It is also important to remember that heavy, thick pieces of clay will make unattractive jewelry.

A second method of making a press mold is to make a model of the desired piece directly from clay or plasticene, and then to finish it with the greatest care. This model is placed face up in the bottom of a small box and covered with about one inch of plaster. When the plaster is set up, the box is removed and the model pulled free from the plaster. The rest of the process is as described above.

There are many good commercial glazes that can be applied to the dried pieces before they have been fired, thus eliminating the two firings usually necessary in ceramic work. If these pieces are to be used as jewelry, the children can use findings (pin backs, clips, and so on) and adhesives made especially for ceramic materials. These are available in hobby stores, art supply stores, and often in dime stores. As in every process described in this book, the design must be something that comes from the child, based upon his experiences and level of development. Never get into ceramic jewelry that copies the poor design of adults. These are generally a misuse of the material.

DECORATIVE PROCESSES: GLAZING, ENGOBES, PRESSING, SGRAFFITO

Clay work can be decorated in a wide variety of ways. The most common way is to glaze the entire piece, after it has had its first, or bisque, firing. For the beginning teacher, commercial glaze, purchased in either moist or dry form, will be most satisfactory. Glazes are silicas that contain other elements, such as oxides, which color them after they are fired. Window glass is a silica; glazes are glasses that make the clay surface both nonporous and visually and tactilely attractive.

Figure 7-16. Clay pipes were popular among tobacco smokers of the last century. The two molds form the right and left sides of a decorated terra cotta pipe bowl. Ceramic molds employ two methods: slip casting and pressing. In slip casting, liquid clay is poured into a plaster mold and allowed to remain long enough for a thick coat to form on the walls. The remainder is poured out. As the clay on the walls of the molds begins to dry it shrinks slightly and loosens. Once free, it is dried completely and later fired. (The Smithsonian Institution)

Figure 7-17. This simple press mold was made by modeling the round face of earth clay, placing it in a small, shallow box, and filling the box with plaster of Paris. When the plaster hardened, the box and the modeled form were removed, leaving the plaster with a reverse impression of the original shape.

Figure 7-18. This seal from ancient India was skillfully carved from a block of steatite, or soapstone. Ancient artists frequently carved familiar animals—such as this elephant—though occasionally the animals were legendary or mythological. (Reproduced courtesy of the Indian Museum, Calcutta)

7-16

7-17

7-18

Glaze can be applied by spraying, dipping, or brushing. Children can finish most beginning work satisfactorily by brushing the moist glaze onto the piece with a soft brush.

Engobes, as described above, are clays in a liquid form, about the thickness of cream, to which oxides or other coloring elements have been added. These can be painted on the surface of clay before it is completely dry; applied by simple stenciling, such as described in Chapter Five; or *slip trailed*, a method of the early Pennsylvania Dutch potter. To slip trail, one fills a small rubber syringe with liquid engobes, which are gently squeezed out onto the clay surface. This is a nice free method for larger pieces, but it is not easily enough controlled for detailed decorations. The early potter also used engobes to cover the entire surface of a piece, after which he used a small sgraffito knife to scratch away portions of the engobe. This scratch, or sgraffito, process is an excellent method for direct expression by children.

Engobe, unlike glaze, does not make the piece nonporous, so a glaze must be applied over the fired piece. The glaze always heightens the colors of the engobes. It is recommended that these be purchased in dry form and mixed in small jars as needed. They mix easily, and the dry materials are easier to store.

Figure 7-19. Red earthenware plate decorated in sgraffito, American (Pennsylvania), 1826. The earliest American pottery was plain red earthenware with little decoration. Later it was decorated with slip and sgraffito. After a piece was formed, a mixture of thin clay, called slip, was used to cover the entire surface or was trailed across part of the piece from a goose quill spout. If the whole surface was covered, designs were scratched through the top layer of slip to expose the darker clay beneath. The potter used traditional designs brought from Europe. When dry, the pieces were fired, then glazed and refired. (The Metropolitan Museum of Art, Gift of Mrs. Robert W. de Forest, 1933)

Figure 7-20. This unusual stoneware pitcher of the early nineteenth century was made for a special presentation. After the potter had thrown a conventional pitcher form on the wheel, he modeled facial features from additional clay and carefully added them to the basic form. He also impressed the name of the donee and the message, in this case, "keep me full." (The Smithsonian Institution)

Figure 7-21. This example of Inca pottery from pre-Columbian America shows a feline animal grasping a man. Made of white clay, this heavy-walled vase was decorated with a red clay pigment. Inca pottery was simple, yet it combined function and design in a highly sophisticated way. (Courtesy of the Musée de l'Homme, Paris)

Figure 7-22. Spout vessel, Peruvian, pre-Incan. One of the most unusual styles in pre-Columbian pottery is the stirrup handle, often made in the shape of fruits, vegetables, small animals, and human heads. As pottery developed, the walls became thinner and the pieces larger. The surfaces were covered with a layer of fine-grained clay colored with siliceous mineral pigments. They were then rubbed smooth with a bone. Often the pottery was decorated with scenes showing the lesser creatures and objects of the world dressed and performing as men. This jar, for example, shows a battle between bean warriors. (Courtesy of the Art Institute of Chicago. Buckingham Fund)

7-19

7-20

7-21

7-22

Children can sometimes greatly enhance the surface of clay by rhythmically impressing patterns into it. Pressing can be done whenever the clay is pliable. Children can find patterns in objects that are handled every day: the head of a screw, a nut or bolt, a twig, a comb, a plastic fork, a dowel stick, natural forms, and so on. The child may wish to cut his own designs from an art gum eraser, a piece of soft wood, or a scrap of linoleum. Pieces of heavily textured fabrics, small screens, chains, or strings can create interesting surfaces. To make tree ornaments, the surface treatments can be used on small circles cut with fruit juice cans that have had both ends removed. Having both ends of the can open makes it possible to push the circles free with a small dowel. Older children can improvise unusual cutters from strips of scrap tin bent and shaped like cookie cutters. Any piece that is to become a hanging ornament should have a small hole, made with a match stick, for a nylon filament or thread for hanging.

KILNS AND FIRING

To fire a piece of ceramic is to heat it to a temperature high enough to change the clay from a fragile soft state to a solid hardened state. If the piece is to have a glaze, it usually must be fired at least two times. The first firing, to harden the clay, as discussed above, is called a bisque firing; the second firing, which fuses a glaze to the clay object, is a glaze firing.

In typical school situations, the teacher who wishes to fire the clay pieces of the students most likely will depend upon a commercially made kiln suitable for school use. These kilns come in many sizes and prices. The most practical for beginning work are top loading electric kilns. These operate on electric current available in most schools and are capable of giving excellent service and long use, if cared for properly. For an elementary school, a kiln with a chamber about 18″ × 18″ × 18″ is adequate. Such a kiln requires 220 volts and special wiring. The kiln should be located in a safe spot, out of the way of children. Usually the kiln should sit on a base of bricks or on a concrete floor. It should stand free of walls to allow air to circulate around it in order to avoid overheating adjacent walls or cupboards.

All kiln makers supply firing instructions that are simple to follow. In purchasing a kiln, a pyrometer and an automatic shutoff are good investments because they will help in the control of the kiln temperature and prevent overheating, which shortens the service life of the kiln. Cones are an added control for temperature. A cone is a small ceramic pyramid that slumps at a specific temperature in the kiln. By observing a cone through the peephole in a kiln, it is possible to tell when the proper firing temperature has been attained. For the teacher who wishes to become more deeply involved in ceramics, a careful examination of one or more books devoted specifically to ceramics or pottery will provide additional kinds of information and in greater detail.

IN CONCLUSION

Do not fire the products of very young children, except for purposes of keeping a record of achievement. Do not fire pieces that have not been done well. Demand good workmanship, careful adherence to recommended procedures, and imaginative and creative use of clay. Avoid stereotyped ashtrays, jewelry, vases, and figurines. Do not let the product take over your teaching and the children's learning. Ceramics lend themselves to the natural creative desires of children. With the improved equipment and facilities of many of the newer schools, ceramics is a pleasant and exciting part of the art program.

Figure 8-1. Phlyake's Comedy Mask. In ancient Greece, actors never appeared on stage without masks. The plays, whether comedies or tragedies, usually reenacted an outstanding deed. The mask itself played an important part in the development of the tragic drama and acting itself. The actor, wearing the mask, lost his identity and became, in his feeling, the character he portrayed. (Museo Nazionale, Taranto)

eight

PAPER-MÂCHÉ MASK-MAKING

Papier-mâché has a very limited tradition as an art medium. Examples of papier-mâché seldom survive for long because of its temporary and perishable nature. It is common in the Orient, where it is used for small objects such as toys; in Mexico, where it is used for large processional and holiday figures as well as toys; and in the United States, where it is used a great deal in creating objects for decorating store windows.

Papier-mâché is paper that has been softened to a pulpy state by moisture and to which paste, sizing, or resin has been added to give it unusual strength and hardness when dry. Although it may seem to be only a quick, inexpensive, temporary, or substitute material, it does have a quality and integrity of its own. It is probably one of the most versatile and useful media for school use. Its only limitations are the limits of its users' imaginations.

A whole new world can be opened up in any classroom through the medium of papier-mâché. Unfortunately, papier-mâché like fingerpaint, has gained the reputation of being messy. However, teachers who have worked in papier-mâché and have organized their procedures have found it most adaptable for use in the classroom. For successful experiences in papier-mâché, the teacher needs only quantities of discarded newspapers, a flour or wallpaper paste, and some bits of string or wire. Many finished papier-mâché projects are painted with ordinary water-based paints, but highly successful finishes come from covering the papier-mâché with colored paper, cotton, burlap, or any other suitable material that can create an interesting surface texture.

Imagine, for instance, a fifth-grade class of about thirty pupils in an ordinary classroom. The group has planned to make a large farm, and each child is interested in making one animal. The teacher and children have decided upon the size they will make each animal, and on the day on which the project is to begin, the teacher has ready an adequate quantity of newspapers. For example, suppose the class decides to make small animals about 8″ long and 5″ to 8″ high. The newspapers have been carefully cut in half so that the sheets are about 12″ × 16″. A large container is filled with paste prepared from wallpaper paste flour, which one makes by placing water in a bucket, slowly sifting wallpaper flour into it, and stirring vigorously. By adding the powder to the water, it is very easy to get the paste the proper, smooth consistency. Wallpaper paste can also be purchased from any hardware or school supply store.

Also ready are about three 12″ lengths of wire for each child. If the teacher is in a rural community, he will find many youngsters who can supply bailing wire, or newsboys who can provide good quantities of wire from their bundles. It is not difficult to get boys to prepare all the wire. In addition, there should be a pan at each desk to contain a small quantity of wallpaper paste, several short lengths of string about 8″ to 10″ long, and if possible, about six pieces of gummed tape of the type used for wrapping bundles.

Then the teacher gives each child a sheet of newspaper with which to cover his desk, while one child distributes half sheets of newspaper, providing each pupil with about a half dozen sheets. Another child passes the sticky paper, another the string and the wire, and the class is ready to begin. The teacher begins with the instructions, and the children follow along step by step.

PAPER COILS AND WIRE

Because of the diversity of interests and abilities within every class, the teacher should begin with a basic idea, from which each child can depart as he sees fit. As in most crafts, it is essential that the teacher provide the children with a sound foundation on which to build. For example, he might ask each of the children to follow along as he describes the process of preparing the framework for an animal.

First, each child places a piece of wire across the width of several sheets of newspaper and makes a tight roll, wrapping tape around the ends so that they do not become unrolled. This process is repeated until all three coils are complete. Now two of the coils are bent double to form legs, which, because of the wire inside, will retain their shape. One pair of legs is slipped over the third coil and fastened in place with bits of string, tape, or a small piece of wire. When this is firm, the second set of legs is placed. Here the child makes the decision. If it is going to be a long, slender animal, like a dachshund, the legs are placed far apart; if it is to be tall and delicate, like a fawn, the legs are placed close together. After both sets of legs are firmly attached to the third coil, the child must decide whether the animal will have a long or short neck, a bulky or light frame, whether it will be seated or standing, and so on. Because of the wire inside of the coil, the children can modify the positions and shapes considerably at this time. They are then encouraged to go on forming additional coils for long necks or heads or wadding up paper and tying it on to give a full, round body. Some children may even decide that one set of legs might better be wings and may wish to remove one set and reverse its position.

Figure 8-2. This display head was used by an early nineteenth-century milliner in Salem, Massachusetts. It was probably built up on a clay or hand-carved wooden form, then cut into two pieces in order to remove it. The pieces were rejoined and the entire papier-mâché heavily coated with gesso or gypsum, sanded smooth, then painted. (The Smithsonian Institution)

8-3

8-4

Now the process is in the hands of the children, and the teacher can only encourage them individually by urging each child to experiment, to seek unique ways of solving problems. Occasionally he may see an opportunity for individual instruction. Gifted children will see a multitude of possibilities and will develop their animals in ways that the teacher never dreamed of, whereas slower children may find it difficult to think much beyond the basic structure and may gain their creative satisfaction from painting or decorating this simple form.

When the children have developed the forms as fully as possible by adding wads, coils, or small pieces, they cover the entire figure carefully with strips of newspaper that have been dipped into the wallpaper paste. Several complete coatings are essential for a good, strong figure. The paste adds considerable strength and gives a hard surface on which to paint. Some teachers like to add a final coat of torn paper toweling for a better painting surface. Although this may be desirable, it is certainly not necessary.

After the figures have been allowed to dry for a number of days, they are painted. The teacher should encourage the children to be experimental in their selection of colors and should not limit them to realistic interpretations. When the teacher is free in his approach, the feeling is contagious, and the children soon learn to work freely and experimentally. While the figures are drying, the teacher should encourage the children to bring in scrap materials that they think might be useful in adding a final touch of decoration to their papier-mâché figures. This search for new uses for old materials is just another part of the teacher's daily job in developing the sensitivity of each child to the world about him. Inventiveness and imaginative thinking are basic to the value of craft teaching.

Learning to follow directions has an important place in the classroom. There are many arts and crafts projects that require a balance between directed and creative activities. Any project that remained entirely directed would have questionable value in the modern classroom. However, if through clear, sound directions, the teacher can help each child get a good foundation on which to build, directed activities are entirely justified. It is foolish to think that materials placed before children and a command or suggestion will suffice as motivation. There will be some children in every classroom who can begin to do creative craft work with minimal motivation, but the teacher who pays attention to individual dif-

---

Figure 8-3. Too often a solid structure appears static. Using a wire armature that is covered later with papier-mâché makes possible a greater feeling of action and movement. (Photograph by Ed Leos)

Figure 8-4. In several countries of the East, papier-mâché toys are common. This delightful toy prancing horse from India is a combination of papier-mâché, wood, gesso, and paint.

ferences is quick to realize that many youngsters would have only failures with this laissez-faire teaching. There is nothing quite so discouraging as a project that falls apart halfway through the lesson because insufficient care or time has been taken during the early steps. Some children may have the patience to begin again, but most become discouraged and are ready to stop. Most teachers are aware of the fact that some children become accustomed to habitual failure and lose all confidence in their work. The teacher needs to pay a great deal of attention to the differences among children and to see that each child gets sufficient encouragement and direction to help him in his project to the point where he can create successfully.

SIMPLE, BULKY FIGURES

The age level at which papier-mâché can be used depends upon the classroom situation. However, it is seldom possible to do successful papier-mâché work below the third grade. With the smallest children, the first experiences in papier-mâché should be limited to simple, bulky figures, such as birds, ducks, rabbits, mice, and the like. Small children might begin by stuffing small paper bags with wads of newspapers to form the main body of the animal and then to make additional small wads of newspaper for the head. They can fasten this head to the first body section by taking long strips of newspaper about an inch wide, dipping them into wallpaper paste, and fastening them across the head and down along the body. This process is repeated until sufficient strips have been used to set the head firmly in place.

Children can create additional appendages from folded paper, if they are to be wings or tails, or from other small wads, if they are to be legs or ears or a nose. They can attach each of the additional appendages by using the long strips of newspaper dipped in paste. Again, the more creative children will think of a multitude of uses for the paper and will develop many variations, whereas the less imaginative child will content himself with a head and body form that he paints

Figure 8-5. Few experiences in life match the true experience of sharing—sharing in learning, in helping, in creating. Art experiences that permit the sharing of ideas, of responsibility, and of success can only contribute to a richer life for all who participate. (Photograph by Donna J. Harris)

Figure 8-6. Learning can take place only when the child can become involved in what is being taught. Thus art is an excellent tool for the achievement of learning, for the child puts himself into creative activities, and the object becomes a part of him. (Photograph by Carl Purcell, National Education Association)

8-5

8-6

or decorates simply. The teacher will consider this a successful creative project if each child has achieved his limits within the project presented.

STAND-UPS

Children in the upper elementary and junior high school grades enjoy making stand-up papier-mâché figures. For this the teacher should have each child bring two metal coathangers, a piece of scrap wood at least 8″ wide and 1″ thick, and some newspapers. Most teachers will make this an assignment for several children to insure that all the materials will be present on the day of the project. The teacher needs a good pair of wire cutters or lineman's pliers, which might be borrowed from the school shop or, if they are not available there, may be brought in by a child. He will need some small metal staples of the type used to attach wire fencing to wooden posts; these should be about 1/2″ in length and can be acquired in any hardware store. The coathangers should be cut in advance by several of the stronger boys. It is impossible to press a wire cutter completely through a coathanger, but it is necessary only to score it with the wire cutters, then bend it, and it will break. These coathangers are then opened up to their fullest length—about 2′–2½′. At one end of each wire the boys can bend a small circular shape that will serve as a foot and provide a good means for stapling the figure to the board.

Each child is given two pieces of wire to staple to the board. At this point he must decide whether the figure may be one that is to stand on one foot, crouch, or kneel. The children fasten the wires the distance apart that they think the feet should be, then make two coils by rolling newspaper. These coils will be as long as

---

Figure 8-7. These figures were built around bottles. The various shapes that bottles come in suggest the many possibilities inherent in them. They are easily obtained; they are easily stored; and they are versatile.

Figure 8-8. An art project may look complete at various stages in its development. Such is the case with this papier-mâché figure of an Eskimo hunter, which awaits its final painting and trim.

Figure 8-9. In Mexico, papier-mâché is widely used to make toy animals and carnival masks. It is also used to make the famous Judas images, such as this one, which are part of the Easter season festivities. These figures, some twice life size, represent death and well-known, unpopular people. On Easter Saturday, fireworks are tied to them and exploded, thus destroying them and symbolically destroying what they represent.

Figure 8-10. Mini-doll by Jane K. Morais. Most often papier-mâché is finished by painting, but this artist carefully covered her papier-mâché doll with a final layer of colored comic strip paper. (Museum of Contemporary Crafts of the American Craftsmen's Council)

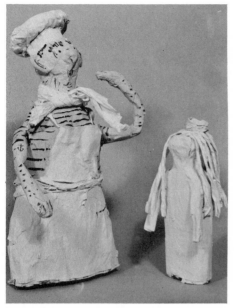

8-7

8-8

8-9   8-10

the coat hangers. They are slipped down over the wires and slid down to the feet. They can be temporarily joined about where the waist of the figure will be, and the upper parts of the coils can be bent around to form the arms. At this point we have a headless figure with two arms and two legs.

Now the child should be encouraged to manipulate, to change, to try to achieve action or to develop a pose compatible with the type of figure that he intends to make. It may be necessary to loosen one of the feet or to change its position. The flexibility of the project at this time lends itself to a great deal of imaginative thinking. At this point the child may make a small third coil, tape a snowball-sized wad to the end of it, slip this coil between the shoulders of the first two coils, and fasten it permanently into place to form the neck and head.

After this, the procedure is the same as with all other papier-mâché. Large wads are added where the figure needs to be bulky, details are added and built up, and finally the entire figure is covered with strips of paper dipped in paste. This project invariably creates a number of new problems, particularly that of dressing the figures. The teacher will be surprised by the great variety of interesting solutions to dressing these figures that the children will come up with, and the variety of scrap materials that the children can discover and put to new use.

Such a project can be very successfully correlated with certain social studies or language units in the elementary school. The figures can make most unusual centerpieces or table decorations for parties or banquets, or can provide fine window displays for many seasonal events.

BOTTLE OR MILK CONTAINER STAND-UPS

An effective smaller stand-up can be made without having to be concerned with improvising a base. Papier-mâché can be used to cover either a bottle, such as a quart vinegar bottle, a plastic bottle, or a quart-sized waxed paper milk container. A little sand poured into the container adds stability to the finished figure. Using paper strips that have been dipped in paste, the student covers the entire container, then slowly builds up the piece by adding papier-mâché in the form of small pulp bits, strips, or paper rolls with wire inserts for arms, with several thicknesses of flat paper pasted together to form ears, wings, and clothing. The methods of papier-mâché are interchangeable, and all can be used on any one piece. The important thing is to use whatever method will give the desired outcome.

These container figures may cause the children to move away from realistic concepts and will result in most imaginative products. This is the kind of project that lends itself well to group work, as the project will place certain limits on the group that will make for a kind of unity. For example, the theme "costumes of all nations" will elicit individual interpretations, but the various treatments will be reasonably similar. It is good to tie some of these projects in with other learning experiences and other subjects.

MINIATURES

In many of our schools, lack of space, especially storage space, is a matter of great concern. In such instances, the teacher may wish to use papier-mâché but keep the projects as small as possible. Many teachers think large size is synonymous with worth or creativity. This is not the case, of course. To do small papier-mâché animals, the teacher might provide each child with about a yard of stovepipe wire, a soft, annealed iron wire available in any hardware store. Its flexibility makes it effective for use by children.

The wire is used for an armature or framework within the papier-mâché. It is best if one builds the entire armature from a single piece of wire, to prevent parts from falling off or slipping out of place. The long piece of wire is bent in half and at the bend is grasped between the thumb and forefinger and twisted for several inches, though as little as possible. This portion will serve as the head and neck parts of the figure. The remaining two wires are separated, and about 5″ along the wire from the last twist, one of the pieces is again bent double and twisted in the same way as the head-neck portion. This forms one of the forelegs or arms. The process is repeated on the other strand of wire, so that both limbs are of the same length. The child wraps the two strands together to form what will be the body section, and at this point decides whether it is going to be a long or short body. After these strands have been twisted for 3″–4″, the strands are again separated, and going out 4″–5″ from the last twist, one strand is folded and twisted to form one of the back legs; using the second strand, the child completes the last leg. There will be short strands left on each side, which the child twists together to form a tail. By bending these sets of legs together, the child should form a wire sculpture that can stand firmly. Children will want to manipulate these, create types of animals or figures—some sitting, some standing, some running—until they are satisfied with a position. Then they can place papier-mâché strips directly over the wire, and build up the figure. These should be neat, compact little papier-mâchés, but should be in every way as well and creatively produced as any of the larger types.

BALLOONS AND PAPIER-MÂCHÉ

Sometimes, for variety, the teacher may want the children to make hollow, or "piggy bank," papier-mâché animals. Variously shaped inexpensive balloons, one for each child, will provide the basis for interesting figures. Children inflate the balloons and very carefully cover them with three or four layers of papier-mâché to form the main figure, and add additional body parts as needed, such as a wad for a head, small wads for legs, or coils for long necks or legs. These papier-mâché figures are developed like the others and when dry are very, very light, but exceedingly strong. Some teachers actually do cut a slot in the back of these so that the children may use them as banks. This procedure can be used to develop such things as papier-mâché globes or planets and will be further described below.

GIANT-SIZED PAPIER-MÂCHÉ FIGURES

Some occasions demand an unusually large papier-mâché. This may be the result of group thinking; children may decide they want a large Santa Claus and reindeer, or a Mexican burro, or perhaps a prehistoric animal. There are absolutely no limitations on the size of a papier-mâché figure, as anyone who has ever seen the large floats in a big parade will testify. Normally, to do a large one in a classroom requires construction of the basic framework using a table or box, modeling the basic shape over it with chicken wire or poultry mesh. This wire screening is very easy to manipulate and can be cut with tin snips or wire cutters. Considerable care must be exercised because of the sharp prongs that remain after the wire has been cut. However, this should not deter the teacher from using wire, for if the children doing the modeling wear gloves, there is little danger.

Once the basic shape has been developed and covered with the chicken wire, children can cover the entire form with large pieces of newspaper dipped in paste. This can be worked out through the use of committees or small groups of individuals working during their free time. If these large figures are made well enough and coated heavily with shellac or varnish after they are completed and perfectly dry, they should be sufficiently waterproof to be placed outdoors for short periods of time, perhaps a week or two. For example, a large Santa or snowman that may

---

Figure 8-11. To insure a perfect fit, a mask can be built over the wearer's face. The face is covered with a piece of cloth. Gummed tape goes under the chin, alongside the cheek, over the top of the head, down the other cheek, and back under the chin. This is repeated several times, then strips are run up, down, and across the front. This basic form is removed and papier-mâché added until the mask is completed. Eye and nose holes are cut when the mask is dry. (Photograph by Ed Leos)

Figure 8-12. Masks have been part of theater for thousands of years. Indeed, the very symbol of the theater is the famous Greek masks of tragedy and comedy, which were worn by players in the Greek theatre to express concretely the general tenor of the play. Masks are particularly well suited to children's plays, for they excite the imagination as few things can. (Photograph by Ed Leos)

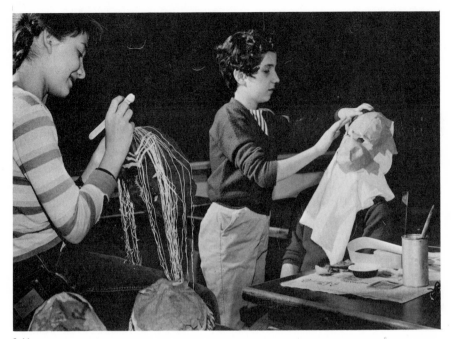

8-11

8-12

have decorated the classroom for several weeks before Christmas could be shel-lacked and placed in the schoolyard during the holidays. It is unimportant if it deteriorates during this period, for its purpose will probably have been fulfilled.

MISCELLANEOUS PROJECTS

There are many times during the school year when one of the regular units of work might be made more meaningful through a special project, such as the development of a model, the making of a relief map, or the building of a diorama. In many instances, papier-mâché may be the material that most easily solves the problem.

MASKS

Masks are among the most universal of art forms. There are few cultures, ancient or modern, primitive or sophisticated, in which masks have not been used. Their use seems to rise from instinctive needs and beliefs common to all men. To under-stand the meaning of masks, one must know their use. In our culture their use has been primarily for fun by children at Halloween and masquerade parties, but the Iroquois Indians of the eastern United States were mask-makers long before the coming of the white settlers. With their masks, the secret Iroquois False Face Society attempted to aid and protect the Iroquois people by warding off evil spirits responsible for disease and by promoting fertility in their crops. To the Indian the mask was a serious art form, as it must have been to the Stone Age men who dressed in the skins and heads of animals for their special ceremonies.

Masks symbolize what they are designed to depict: animals, heroes, characters in a drama, wind, rain, supernatural beings, spirits of good and evil, ancestors, gods, spirits of nature, and so forth. They have been used for satire and buffoonery, for terrorizing others, as emblems of special groups, to cause laughter or fear, to cure disease, and to impersonate people or supernatural beings. In some countries an actor never appears onstage without a mask. In Japan, India, and Greece the mask continues to be widely used in traditional theatre.

The teacher should capitalize on this universality to make a classroom project with masks that will both provide a means for personal self-expression for each of the children and at the same time develop a better understanding of other cultures and peoples.

Any craft project that is done simply for the sake of doing it or of acquiring certain skills is of questionable value. In no case should the teacher allow the product to become an end in itself, for creative work in crafts must be meaningful to have educational value. Each project should be thought through sufficiently to provide for as many of the basic objectives of education, and specifically art education, as possible. Every good teacher knows that we begin with children as they are and seek to broaden their horizons only as rapidly as they are able to assimilate meaningful material. Therefore, when we start making masks with our smallest children, we should do so with reference only to those things that might have meaning to them. They would understand masks most through their experiences with Halloween parades and parties, so this would be the logical point of departure. Later, as their interests and understanding broaden, the teacher would refer to masks in the North American culture of United States Indians, Canadian Indians, and Eskimos, and as their horizons expand, the teacher would discuss the cultures of other countries and point out the significance of masks in each of the cultures.

PAPER BAG MASKS

The easiest way to start making masks is for the teacher or students to acquire a sufficient number of large paper bags so that each child can have one large enough to slip over his head. If these are very large, it might be desirable to cut an inverted U-shape from each of the two sides, so that the bag can slip down over the child's shoulders. The child can locate the position of his eyes, and with a crayon gently mark for eye openings on the bag. Next comes cutting and pasting, developing eyes, nose, mouth, hair, and ears as completely as each child is capable of doing. One must not discourage deviation from reality, for with small children such deviation is normal. Green noses and purple lips are commonplace and should be accepted. Children can easily decorate paper bag masks with crayons if they have used paper and paste frequently or if these materials are unavailable. Sometimes a bit of raffia, shavings from the wood shop, strands of yarn, or a piece of ribbon can be used to set off the finished mask. The teacher should keep a box of these interesting materials in the classroom. Even the smallest children will quickly find appropriate uses for them in their constructions. A milk bottle cap will soon become a nose or a scrap of colored cellophane a hair ribbon. This type of mask is easily produced in one period and always proves to be a source of fun and stimulation for the children.

PAPER PLATE MASKS

Paper plate masks are good to try in the middle elementary grades. To give them a three-dimensional quality, the children cut two slits about 2″ deep and 2″ or 3″

8-13

8-14

8-15

8-16

apart in the edge of the plate. Overlapping the sides adjacent to each slit slightly and stapling them back together, forms a simple chin cup, which makes the mask fit nicely. The child can locate and mark the position of his eyes and later, with the point of the scissors, make incisions for them. The teacher might illustrate methods by which the nose can be cut on the bottom and two sides and flapped out for an interesting three-dimensional quality, or how a hole might be cut in the center where the nose normally would be, or how other types of noses, such as a cone, pyramid, box, or simply a crumpled wad, can be developed from construction paper.

These first experiments in three-dimensional paper sculpture will lead to interesting improvisations for eyebrows, hair, cheeks, and ears. The teacher should encourage the children at this point to experiment with the paper in as many ways as possible and to develop the masks as a project in paper sculpture. The child can ornament the edges of the paper with feathers, fur, cotton, or hair to get interesting effects for the type of mask he is making. Again, a scrap box with such things as raffia, yarns, shavings, and steel wool will be invaluable for suggesting new and different approaches to making masks. If these materials are not available, paint and crayons can suffice to make very interesting masks. Finally, a rubber band can be stapled to each side and slipped around the child's head to hold the mask in place.

Whenever possible, the teacher ought to encourage children to be inventive

---

Figure 8-13. Helmet and half-mask with gorget, Japanese, eighteenth century. The Japanese created armor much like that of medieval Europe. It was highly decorated and generally grotesque, and was so well made that a suit might last for generations. The terrifying decoration is similar to the expressionism characteristic of Japanese art, because the armorers worked closely with artists, especially painters. (Reproduced courtesy of The Metropolitan Museum of Art, New York. Gift of Bashford Dean, 1914)

Figure 8-14. The Iroquois Indians were the best mask-makers of the area included by the United States. They made two major types of masks, carved wooden ones known as Falsefaces and braided cornhusk masks, known as Huskfaces. Both of these were made before the coming of the white man. The cornhusk masks were used in ceremonies to promote success with their crops and the carved masks were used by the Falseface society to appeal to the evil spirits responsible for sickness and disease. (Museum of the American Indian. Heye Foundation)

Figure 8-15. Javanese mask. Religious and aesthetic attitudes often inspired the most humble handiwork of the Orient. Creative expression was thought to be in some way a manifestation of life, which in itself was considered holy. (The Smithsonian Institution)

Figure 8-16. Eskimo Mask. The majority of Eskimo masks were used as a means of contacting the spirits, such as the spirit of sickness or the spirit of winter. Other masks were used for ceremonies and for entertainment—even a form of caricature. Their styles varied greatly in their efforts to create animal, imaginary, and human masks. Grotesqueness, as in this asymmetric mask is common, as is the use of decorative materials such as feather, hair, bone, or animal fur. (National Film Board of Canada. Photograph by Gar Lunney)

Figure 8-17. Occasionally the spontaneous project—the instant mask, costume, or banner— is the most successful because it occurs at a period when interest is at its peak and the enthusiasm of the children says, "Do it now!" (Photograph by Ed Leos)

by asking them to create a mood or a feeling, to make the mask look "mean" or look "sad" rather than to make it look "real."

BALLOON MASKS

A balloon that can be inflated larger than a child's head makes an unusual base for large and interesting masks. After it is inflated, the balloon is covered with three or four carefully applied layers of papier-mâché and put aside to dry. Then the children can begin to develop the type of mask they want. Using the standard methods of papier-mâché figure making, they can develop whatever creature they wish from this basic, round shape. When the papier-mâché has dried and hardened, the teacher, using a razor blade or X-acto knife, must cut a hole in the bottom of the mask large enough for the child to slip his head through. The balloon may then be removed. Eye openings can easily be disguised when the mask is painted. This kind of mask would probably be best decorated with a good-quality poster or tempera paint, and then decorated with bits of scrap materials.

This same procedure can be used to make globes, moons, or planets.

GUMMED PAPER MASKS

One of the most effective and best-fitting masks, which should be done in the upper elementary grades, requires the use of a quantity of gummed kraft tape, tissue paper or cloth, and papier-mâché. This project is generally begun with a demonstration. A variety of lengths of gummed tape, from 6″ to 2′ are ready for the demonstration, and a piece of paper towelling that has been soaked in water is ready for moistening the tape. The teacher begins by placing the piece of cloth or paper over the child's face and hair. Then, with a 2-foot-long piece of moistened tape, he carefully goes around from under the chin up over the top of the head, forming an oval. This is pressed down firmly and the process is repeated several times. Now shorter strips are run from one side of the face to the other, joining the oval from side to side. Next some of the strips are run from top to bottom. By now a definite, half-spherical form has been developed that actually has the shape of the head. It can be removed and wadded newspaper placed inside it to give added strength, and the teacher can demonstrate how, through the use of sticky paper, much of the basic shape can be developed before starting with the papier-mâché. For example, short strips can be buckled and very carefully built up to any size or shape to form a nose, eyebrows, eyes, mouth, or chin. When

Figure 8-18. One of the famous remaining folk masquerade carnivals is held in the Wallis Canton of Switzerland. Here, a group wearing frightening masks and dressed in sheepskins, with many bells tied to their belts, create noise and excitement. In the German, Austrian and Swiss Alps, the people excel as mask-makers. (Schweizerisches Museum für Völkskunde, Basel)

the basic shape has been developed, the child can go to work, using papier-mâché strips and pieces.

After the teacher's demonstration, the children pair off and repeat this process on each other until each has his own fitted mask to develop. The teacher should be careful to lay a good groundwork for the understanding of masks. He may have illustrations of primitive masks on the bulletin board, or may have shown a film. This background will help to break down certain stereotypes that might otherwise prevail. Excess cloth is removed, excess tissue paper cut away, and the masks can be painted and decorated as in other projects.

This particular type of mask can be used very effectively in small dramas that the children can develop themselves. The masks can even be mounted on long sticks painted black, and the children can work out very exciting plays against a black background, using a darkened room and a floodlight to light the stage. The children can keep out of sight by kneeling behind a table and can manipulate their mask heads against the black background for a most appealing performance.

These procedures are only a few of the many possibilities in making masks. They are, however, the well-tried, basic ones and can be a starting point for many variations that the teacher may wish to try.

Figure 9-1. Painted tapa from the Fiji Islands with a branch and leaf design. Tapa, or bark cloth, is a lightweight paper-like fabric made from the inner bark of trees. It has been used for clothing, masks, bedding, and funeral wrappings. Making tapa is a primitive art restricted to the tropic areas. The designs are usually similar to those found in the carvings and paintings of that particular culture. (Museum für Völkekunde, Hamburg)

nine

FABRICS

Necessity is the mother of invention, and many crafts had their origins in the needs of primitive man. The need to have vessels in which to store food, to have tools with which to build shelters, and to have clothing with which to protect the body from heat and cold all contributed to the discovery of crafts. As the primary problems were met, these crafts gained both functional and aesthetic refinements.

Furs and hides served as the first clothing, and fabrics soon followed them. Early man was extremely ingenious in developing the first looms, for he discovered at the outset the principle of weaving, which has never been changed, only modified, in thousands of years. He devised a loom that was probably made of two sticks to serve as a frame to hold parallel threads, called the warp, through which other threads, the weft, could be woven back and forth to make fabric. He did the weaving by picking up alternate threads of the warp with his fingers and running the weft under them, creating the basic over-and-under rhythm of the weaving process. The first weavers, like the primitive weavers of today, probably tied this simple frame between two trees or hung one end from a low branch and tied the other to their waists.

As man mastered the fundamental processes, his urge to decorate led him into various weaving modifications, including the introduction of color, pattern, texture, and new materials. The weavers of today are still vigorously exploring exciting possibilities. Materials never thought to be in the province of the fabric maker are continually being introduced. When fabrics became commonplace, artists began to use the surface of the fabrics for decorating with additional, or applied, fabric. This process was called *appliqué*. Or they chose to enrich the surfaces with threads in a process called *embroidery*. As artists, they worked with color, form, and texture to create their designs.

Fabrics present a new experience to the child, for it is with them that he begins to sense textile structure by touch as well as sight. The child should be offered tactile experiences with various kinds of yarns, fibers, threads, reeds, and natural materials, all of which might ultimately be useful in weaving or appliqué. It is in the use of these materials and in the ultimate choices and combinations he must make that the child becomes actively involved in design. Although he may approach it in an informal or even unconscious way, he nonetheless organizes his

9-2

9-3

Figure 9-2. Early Nazca embroideries from the coastal region of Peru, ca. 200–400 A.D. This fabric was part of a garment with a slit used as a neck opening. It is embroideried with a design of buzzard-like birds. Because of the custom of placing an assortment of garments and cloths in tombs, most Andean textiles have come from graves. The Peruvians made their fabrics from cotton, alpaca, llama, and vicuña. (The Metropolitan Museum of Art. Gift of George D. Pratt, 1933)

Figure 9-3. Queen of Sheba Admiring the Wisdom of Solomon, American (Massachusetts), 1744. This polychrome petit-point representation of a biblical story demonstrates how artists can draw upon their knowledge, experience, and imagination. Note how the biblical figures are dressed in the style of the eighteenth century and how the landscape, carriages, and homes are typically colonial American.

9-4

9-5

Figure 9-4. Fragment from the Baldishoel Tapestry, Norway, ca. 1180. Considered to be the most important example of historic Norwegian tapestry, this bench covering from an early church depicts the months of April and May. Tapestries are figured hand-woven fabrics usually of wool and used as wall hangings or furniture coverings. (Kunstindustrimuseet, Oslo)

Figure 9-5. Model of a weaving shop, Egyptian, Middle Kingdom. It was customary to place carefully made models of essential crafts in the tombs of the deceased dignitaries for use in after life. This wood model of a simple horizontal loom, about $8\frac{1}{2}$″ high, was stuccoed and painted. The weaving process it depicts is essentially the same as the loom used today for carpets and tapestry. (The Metropolitan Museum of Art, New York. Anonymous gift, 1930)

ideas and develops a plan or design. He decides to repeat or not to repeat, to use bright or subdued colors, to use large motifs or small. All these are decisions relating to his design; when he is able to incorporate all of them into a harmonious whole, he is designing.

A SIMPLE WOODEN LOOM

To construct a good, simple loom requires only four pieces of wood, some finishing nails, and some string. Begin with two strips of wood about 3/4″ × 1 1/2″ × 12″, and two pieces 16″ to 18″ long. Nail the two short pieces to the two longer pieces to form a rectangular frame. Drive several nails into each corner of the frame to make it strong. At half-inch intervals down the center of the top of the short strips, drive inch-long finishing nails halfway into the wood and slant them toward the outside of the loom. The loom is now ready to be strung, or "warped."

Tie your string to any corner nail. Stretch it to the opposite side and go around the back of *two* nails, bring it back again and loop it behind nails number two and three, then back to the opposite side, and so on until you have completed stringing the loom. This will place the warp threads parallel at half-inch intervals, making it reasonably easy for the children to use them. Use cotton roving or heavy cotton rug yarn about 1/4″ in diameter and cut it into lengths about 4″ longer than the outside strings on the loom. If these are precut and piled freely in the box, the child can select the colors that are most pleasant to him and can begin to weave on one end. It takes only minutes to explain the process of weaving so the children understand it. When the weaving is complete, packed firm and tight, it can be removed from the loom. At this time the teacher or one of the mothers should stitch each end on a sewing machine. The ends can be trimmed neatly with shears, and the child is the proud possessor of a fine wall hanging.

The same principles just described could be used on a piece of cardboard; notches cut in each end are used to hold the string. Since this would be a smaller loom, the notches would be placed about 1/4″ apart, and finer yarn and a needle could be used for weaving. A tongue depressor or ice cream stick slipped under the warp at each end of this loom will lift the warp from the cardboard and make it a great deal easier for the child to use.

SODA STRAW LOOM

A fine bookmark or belt can be made using soda straws for a loom. Give each child about six straws and six pieces of heavy wool or cotton yarn about 2′ long.

9-6

9-7

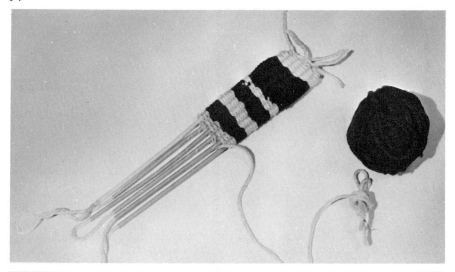

Figure 9-6. Weaving can be done on any frame sturdy enough to stand the tension of the warp. This loom is made of pine. Finishing nails, spaced evenly, are put into each end board, and the warp is strung around them. (Photograph by Ed Leos)

Figure 9-7. A simple loom can easily be constructed of plastic soda straws and yarn. Its convenient size makes it a desirable project to be kept in the students' desks for work in free moments. (Photograph by Ed Leos)

He threads the yarn through each straw by tying a bit of thread to the center of each piece of yarn and pulling the yarn through the straws, so that each has a loop appearing out of one end and two loose ends appearing out of the other. He takes the twelve loose ends and ties them together as a tassel; then, using another piece of yarn for weaving, he holds the six straws together and begins an over-and-under process. When the sixth straw is reached, he simply loops the yarn over and works it back; when the first straw is again reached, the process is repeated. When the weaving is long enough, the straws are slipped out one by one and the looped ends of the yarn tied together in another tassel.

To make a belt in this way, it is necessary to use much longer lengths of yarn, but the process is essentially the same. However, when the soda straws are about three-quarters covered with weaving they are slipped through, leaving only about a quarter of their length still covered, to allow the student to cover another portion before moving the straws again. The process is repeated until the entire length of the yarns have been woven.

CARDBOARD PURSE LOOM

In the upper elementary grades, children can use the cardboard purse loom very effectively to make handsome purses. These can be made in any size or shape but, for our purposes, a purse 5″ × 8″ will be described. Each child is given a piece of cardboard 6″ × 8″. Holding this piece horizontally on the desk, from the top edge he measures down 1/2″ from each of the two top corners and marks. He joins these marks with a line, and does exactly the same thing at the bottom. He now has a cardboard with two horizontal lines running across it, one 1/2″ from the top and the other 1/2″ from the bottom. Then he places a ruler along each of these lines and carefully marks each quarter inch. Using the ruler, he draws lines on the top and bottom, reaching from the half-inch mark to the edge of the cardboard on each quarter-inch marking. Scissors are used to cut these down exactly to the half-inch mark. The cardboard now should appear with rows of notches, top and bottom, 1/2″ deep.

Now to string the loom. If the teacher has ordinary cotton warp available, this is excellent; kite string or other string about that weight is also excellent. The color is immaterial. The child ties one end of this string to the first tab in the upper left-hand corner of the cardboard, using a simple loop and knot to attach it. Then he brings the warp down the front of the cardboard and through the first notch at the bottom. This puts the string at the back of the loom. Going up the back and into the first notch at the top, he makes a complete trip around the loom, returning to the spot where he started. Now the warp is hanging down the front

9-8

Figure 9-8. A cardboard or soft plastic cylindrical container is easily adapted to make a loom. The one principle to remember is to end up with an odd number of strings (warp) even if one must be added after the warping is complete.

of the loom. The child loops it into notch number two at the top, and now it is hanging down the back of the loom. He takes it through notch number two at the bottom and up the front to notch number two at the top. When the warp is taken through notch number two at the top, it is again at the back of the loom. The child loops it into notch number three at the top, and then it is hanging down the front of the loom. He brings it down the front into notch number three at the bottom, takes it through notch number three to the back, and returns again to notch number three at the top, bringing the warp through to the front. He loops it again into notch number four down the back and into notch number four at the bottom, up the front, and into notch number four at the top. By this time the sequence should be clear. The warped strings run parallel, front and back; loops appear at the top at alternate spaces, both front and back.

When the loom is completely strung across to the last notch, front and back, the leftover string will be at the top of the loom. It is then necessary to create one additional warp for the weaving to progress properly. Therefore, the child goes down once more to the bottom corner and ties the string to the last tab, the same way as at the beginning. This makes one notch with a double warp on one side only. Later, during weaving, these two warps will be used separately in the same way as any other two warps on the loom would be.

To insure that the tabs will not be broken during the weaving process, it is a good idea to use a strip of gummed, Scotch, or masking tape on both rows of tabs, front and back.

A good weaving needle can be made from an ice cream stick or half a tongue depressor, split lengthwise, which has been sharpened and sandpapered and into which a small hole has been drilled for the yarn to be inserted. It is important to make a good weaving needle, because it simplifies the work and makes it progress much more rapidly. Using a needle threaded with about a yard of yarn, the child begins near the middle of the loom at the bottom, runs the yarn under about three or four strings, and begins the over-and-under process. When the last string is reached, the child should check whether it was over or under. He turns the loom over and continues around the end, keeping the same sequence of over-and-under as on the front. When finally the double warp is reached, it must be treated as two separate strings. The child goes over one, under the second, and continues the sequence around and around until the yarn has reached its end. He tucks the re-maining bit of yarn under the warps, rethreads the needle, runs it under three or four lines, and begins again. It is undesirable to tie the different pieces of yarn toge-ther. The loose ends will be hidden inside and will never pull out.

When the weaving has reached the top, the teacher should make certain that it is being packed down carefully with a comb or the fingernails or a fork. It should be packed so tightly that none of the warp appears through it. The last few rows will have to be done with a steel darning needle, so that they can be filled as com-pletely as possible. When no more weaving can be done, the tabs are torn off top and bottom. At the top, the loops will open up and the cardboard can be slipped out. Both sides and the bottom will be finished, and the purse will be complete. This project is so popular that once it is begun, some of the children will finish three or four purses. Each time they will seek to do a better job than on the one before, and the quality of this product is almost always very high. Design is limited with this type of loom, and almost always consists of horizontal lines and changes of color or texture. However, after one or two projects, some children will devise unusual techniques for making designs.

For the smaller children, tape with snaps may be sewed in, or they may wish to have help at home in lining the purse. With the older children, the lining is more important, and perhaps a zipper can be inserted for a fine finish.

Some teachers question the advisability of sending a project home with the child for additional help by a parent, but there are times when such an approach is very desirable. There is no better way for a parent to gain insight into the child's way of thinking and the value of art for children than through participating in a project that is very important and meaningful to the child.

OATMEAL OR SALT BOX LOOM

The teacher who understands the procedure of the purse loom can demonstrate a splendid modification, using an oatmeal box or salt box in place of the flat cardboard. Here the markings are made around the top and bottom of the box. It is strung by tying one end of a string to one of the notches at the top, going down to the bottom, across the bottom, and directly up the other side, into a notch, looped over into the next notch, down the side, across the bottom, and up the other side. A few minutes of experimenting with this will easily show how to string this loom. Actually, it is considerably easier than the cardboard loom, for the child does not turn over the loom when he reaches the end. The child simply weaves around and around until he reaches the top, where he tears off the tabs, loosens the loops and removes the cardboard box (or partially removes it), trims it, and reinserts it to help the weaving keep its shape. This type of loom offers a large variety of possibilities. Excellent drawstring purses can be made, interesting modifications of which consist in making short purses and sewing a tube of corduroy or velveteen to the top.

HOOKING

Rug hooking offers the teacher another opportunity to allow the children to design for a purpose. Rug hooking generally begins with a design conceived in chalk or thick tempera or torn colored paper. Teachers should encourage the same freedom in developing designs as they would in free painting or drawing. When a child creates a design that is not too detailed to be worked out, he can nail a hooking frame together from strips of wood, or he may use an old picture frame or sturdy embroidery hoops as the frame. A piece of burlap bag is stretched across the frame and stapled or tacked firmly to it, and the sketch for the design is applied with a crayon. Hooking can be done with yarns or thrums, strips of stocking that have been dyed, strips of rags, or strips of wool jersey. The hooking is done with a crochet hook, available in any dry goods or dime store.

9-9

9-10

The process of hooking is simple. The child holds the yarn or strips of rags beneath the burlap in one hand, inserts the crochet hook through the burlap, catches it into the strip, and pulls the yarn up into a loop on the top. The needle goes through the burlap the second time, hooking the strand again and pulling it up. After a dozen or so strokes, the person hooking learns to judge the proper distance along the strand at which to attach the hook so that each loop is uniform in height. The hooking is done in sufficient closeness to pack the loops in so they will not pull out. The different types of rags and wools will produce different types of textured areas of color and of pile, and as this occurs, the children will modify their designs. The project remains creative to the end. As the child hooks, he will create problems for himself, but he will also discover their solutions.

Also available is an excellent hooking tool that costs about a dollar. This tool is easily threaded with yarn and is used from the back side of the fabric. The tool, which has a sharpened point, is pushed through the burlap or hooking fabric, withdrawn, and pushed through again and again. Each time the point of the tool passes through the fabric one loop remains on the reverse side. This is a very effective means of hooking, in which a good rate of speed is attainable. This tool also permits variations in the height of the loops and the use of several thicknesses of yarn. This is the more desirable way to hook if the project is large.

When a project is finished, the back can be coated with a commercial rubberized liquid to hold all the loops in place, but this is not necessary. The remaining burlap edges can be turned under and sewed into place. Although children are encouraged in the beginning to work on small mats, they usually will want to go on to a larger rug. Rug hooking can be a fascinating experience if it is approached creatively both in design and construction. It can be tedious, however, if it is a purely mechanical process based on commercially prepared designs.

STITCHERY AND EMBROIDERY

To embroider is to ornament with needlework. Most people think of embroidery as busywork done by housewives to ornament towels, handkerchiefs, blouses,

Figure 9-9. This delightful hooked rug by Rose Treat illustrates how simplicity and a carefully thought out grouping of shapes and shades can mean a well-designed product. (Reproduced courtesy of the artist)

Figure 9-10. Appliqued Cotton Quilt, Ca. 1855. Rebecca Diggs chose her motifs from the 1840 presidential campaign of William Henry Harrison, in which "Tippecanoe and Tyler Too" was the slogan. The famous "log cabin" and "cider barrell" appear in the second row. (The Smithsonian Institution)

and so forth. Few people have ever really thought of embroidery as an art form. But it is an old craft, used by the ancient Egyptians and even described in the Old Testament. Its earlier use was primarily to decorate wearing apparel. As a craft it has flourished primarily in peasant cultures and is most often thought of as a peasant art. In twentieth-century America, embroidery has generally been looked upon as a housewife's pastime. In recent years, however, it has suddenly been revitalized, and many people are using it as a pure art form. Beautiful examples are to be found, particularly in churches.

The needlework that was done when grandmother was a child generally consisted of samplers, fancy doilies, and prepared tapestry designs. The emphasis was placed entirely upon making neat and acccurate stitches and carefully following the prepared color arrangements and stamped patterns. This sort of meticulous busywork would give little satisfaction or be of little value to the children of today, who need and demand to be challenged by problems for which they can seek their own solutions. Today's approach to stitchery should be exploratory in nature. The teacher should try to provide the materials best suited to the age of the children, and to provide an atmosphere suitable for creative work. To learn to copy is one thing; but to be original, to follow one's own plan, to keep one's own ideas flowing, to think, to decide, to change, to be filled with the excitement of unknown possibilities ahead, to develop a plan and a design and then to execute it, this is creativity.

With the young child working on loosely woven materials, such as burlap or monk's cloth, and with large tapestry needles and many-colored yarns, the teacher may begin by asking some simple questions: "What can you do with these yarns?" "What can you do to make your materials gay and beautiful?" "Who can think of a stitch to make?" Through these initial experiments, the child can discover that his needle can go in and out, under and over, over three and under one, under three and over one. Soon his resourcefulness will help him invent stitches and select and combine colors that are as personal as the lines and colors he uses in his paintings. In his needlework, the child will most likely develop in his ability to work in the same way he does in his drawing and painting, beginning first with simple lines, then creating areas or shapes, and finally creating textures and surfaces. He will probably begin in a rather unorganized fashion and work toward an organized design, just as he did in painting. As his designs develop on the material, he may occasionally find it necessary to bring in an accent, like a small bit of felt or a bead or an artificial pearl, to develop his ideas to the fullest. As in other crafts, the slow child may limit his thinking to simple, running lines, whereas the more creative child will quickly get the feel of the material and develop beautiful color relationships, textures, and a variety of stitches.

As needlework develops from the lower to the upper grades, the variety of

Figure 9-11. Embroidery was for a long time a neglected art, because it had become mere busy work dependent upon patterns created by others. Today, however, young craftsmen are using it in the most imaginative ways. The availability of materials and their ease of handling and storing are among the reasons why embroidery is regaining popularity in the classroom. (photograph by Carl Purcell, National Education Association)

projects widens. The first projects may be purely decorative or pictorial wall hangings, but later on material can be used for crayon bags, purses, knitting bags, and even large group projects such as curtains or drapes. The opportunities with embroidery are limitless, and one needs only to try it once to discover the many possibilities that it holds.

BATIK

In Ceylon and other Asian countries, many women conduct small household industries as "batikers," or makers of hand-decorated fabrics of unusual beauty. Using the finest cotton or silk, the batiker first washes and softens the cloth, then, using a small copper "tjanting" tool, applies a carefully prepared decoration. This tool, shaped like a small cup with a spout attached, contains heated beeswax, which flows through the spout onto the cloth as it is guided over the surface. When the entire design is covered, the fabric is dipped into a bath of cold dye, generally blue. When it has been in the dye bath for a sufficient length of time, it is removed, dried, and the wax removed by a warm water scrubbing. A second coat of wax is applied, this coat being of a heavier and harder consistency. The second application takes on another design form, covering parts of the first design and parts of the dyed areas. Traditionally, the second dye is brown. When dried, the wax is again removed, and the fabric is covered with a pattern of browns, blues, blue-browns, and the original fabric color. The process can be repeated for additional dyes, but two usually suffice.

It is possible for children to make exquisite batiks in a similar manner, but using much less time and equipment. A supply of bristle and hair brushes is needed to apply wax to the fabrics. Have each child obtain a piece of cotton fabric, such as muslin, about 20″ square or larger. A hotplate, a cookie sheet of steel or aluminum, a muffin tin, and several plastic basins or buckets will be needed. Prepare

---

Figure 9-12. Detail of a Javanese batik. The batiks of Java excel in their design and aesthetic appeal. Based upon patterns of flowers, plant life, and nature, they are highly stylized and individualized. The resist-dying technique of batik is found also in India, Thailand, China and Japan. (The Smithsonian Institution)

Figure 9-13. Lace Construction by Luba Krejei. The work of this superb Czechoslovakian artist merges the skill and patience of the traditional needlecrafts with the inventiveness and freshness of the contemporary craftsman. (Museum of Contemporary Crafts of the American Craftsmen's Council)

Figure 9-14. The contemporary American craftsman has found expressive outlets in both traditional and modern materials and in combinations of the two. This piece by Marilyn Pappas is an example of embroidery and applique executed in a highly individual way. The effect is very much like that of an abstract painting. (Courtesy of Marilyn Pappas)

9-12

9-13

9-14

a work space in one corner of the classroom where a few children can work at one time. Cover the table with wrapping paper or newspaper. The children can work out their ideas for batik designs using large, soft chalks on newsprint. When the designs are ready, the pieces of fabric can be taped to large pieces of cardboard cut from the sides of cartons. Fill each section of the muffin tin with small pieces of crayons, all reds in one, blues in another, yellows in another, and so forth. With the muffin tin resting on the cookie sheet and the cookie sheet on the hot plate, the crayons are slowly melted. The quantity can be increased by the addition of equal parts of beeswax and paraffin. The children can begin painting directly on the fabrics, using brushes dipped in the melted wax as in encaustic painting, described in Chapter Five.

When the painting is complete and the wax hardened, some of the larger areas can be broken or crumbled to create fine hair cracks through which the dye will seep to produce unusual effects. Ordinary cold-water dyes, such as those found in drugstores or dime stores, are mixed in the buckets according to the package directions. The fabrics are dipped and remain in the dye according to the time prescribed by the particular brand, usually twenty minutes to a half hour. These should be hung on a clothesline by their edges, not draped, as draping will create an unwanted stripe as the dye is absorbed by the line. When completely dry, the fabric is placed between layers of newspapers and pressed with a hot iron to melt out the wax. It is essential that the newspapers be changed frequently, as the wax gets absorbed in the paper. With such batiks, it is usually possible to remove most of the wax so that no further cleaning is necessary. Unlike the batiks of the Ceylonese, which leave the waxed areas in the natural color of the fabric, these batiks have pigment in the areas where the colored crayon scraps were used, and are thus multicolored although only a single dye has been used. The children often enhance the pressed batiks by carefully mounting them on cardboard and preparing a mat or cardboard frame to place over them.

APPLIQUÉ

Appliqué is a process whereby pieces of one fabric are sewed or pasted onto another. The fact that small children love to sew and that most homes have large quantities of scrap rags of various colors and sizes makes appliqué an interesting and handy craft project for the elementary school. Since appliqué deals primarily with shapes and flat areas, designs can be worked out with colored paper in advance of the actual cutting and sewing.

Once again the teacher must consider the subject. To approach this new process only through the use of the materials may produce a skillfully done but unimaginative appliqué. We want to encourage children to use the materials inventively and spontaneously, but we also want them to use their imaginations and their perceptions to arrive at a subject for their appliqué. They should be directed to look at the environment, both natural and man-made; to look through a microscope; to look at some of the other children's paintings; *but to look and think first.* As an idea comes and the child begins, the materials will surely suggest new ideas and directions. Once he has decide upon the design, he can select pieces of material to match the colored paper and cut them to size, pin them onto the basic cloth or burlap, and sew them into place. It is always wise for the teacher to encourage the children to make changes as they go along, keeping the project spontaneous to the very end. Changing from paper to cloth may suggest new ideas, and the use of a particular stitch on the edge may suggest another. Even the addition of stitches over portions of the cloth may create new textures and solve problems that arise.

Appliqué can be used for wall hangings or drapes, aprons, or purses. If the teacher is near a large city, he can probably acquire great quantities of wonderful scrap cloth by visiting dress factories, and excellent felt scraps from hat manufacturers. Sometimes this material is simply thrown away or burned, and it can be had for the asking. When the teacher is able to acquire a quantity of felt hat scraps, he may find many useful applications in the making of mittens, slippers, headbands, comb cases, glasses cases, and purses. The felt can be used as appliqué on all the needlework projects mentioned above. Lack of classroom materials should not be considered a handicap but a challenge.

Good art programs are always built on ingenuity, initiative, and imaginative use of scrap materials. One can seldom attribute a poor arts or crafts program to a lack of anything other than the teacher's own resourcefulness. Work in fabrics is not something that can be hurried into and finished in one class period. It requires careful planning, a background of rich, related information, and a patient approach. Children begin school with short interest spans, which increase as the child moves toward maturity. Activities that help to develop increasing interest spans and perseverance are essential to the child's healthy development. We err when we take the fast and easy approach to everything and allow children to develop careless habits. Well-planned projects that result in well-designed and well-made products can only help the child in his total development.

10-1

ten

POTPOURRI

This chapter includes projects that could fit into several categories in the earlier chapters. They are grouped here because none is sufficiently long to warrant a separate chapter.

BUILDING WITH BOXES

At the back of every store, in the basement of every school, in the garage of every home are empty cardboard boxes waiting for small children with big ideas to turn them into houses, trains, automobiles, or buses. If the classroom has a corner that needs a special project, the class need only gather together a half dozen or so cardboard cartons of various sizes to start a project. After discussing what to make, the children may decide to build a train; the largest box becomes the engine, another the tender, and others a freight car, a passenger car, and a caboose. Using tempera paints and large brushes, the children quickly and easily plan and paint their train, and soon it is all assembled and tied together with pieces of roving or rope. The following day during library period, some of the children can sit in the train to read their books. This project is always imaginative and easy, and it takes little motivation on the part of the teacher to make it highly successful.

Waxed cardboard quart containers can also be accumulated and used in a variety of ways. By cutting them in different ways, the children can make trains, cars, tables, or cupboards and may even turn some of them into heads or people. Brass fasteners and a stapler are very handy to have for this kind of construction.

MOSAICS

Mosaics are surface decorations made of small pieces of colored glass, stone, or other inlaid materials. The simplest mosaics for the elementary school are made

Figure 10-1. Some toys such as doll houses, dolls, puppets, miniature furniture, vehicles, and household utensils are models because they reproduce accurately larger objects. The expertness of the craftsman combined with the careful documentation of historical styles make some worthy of museum exhibition. (Milwaukee Public Museum)

of small bits of torn colored paper. If the colored paper scrap box seems to be getting full, the teacher may have some of the children cut it into half-inch-square pieces on the paper cutter. If possible, the children should make an effort to keep the colors separate by placing the pieces in different small boxes, such as cigar boxes. When a sizable quantity of pieces have been cut, the class may try a mosaic picture. It would be good to bring in illustrations of mosaics done in the early Byzantine churches or of some contemporary works, so that the children can understand better the meaning of the project; every lesson in crafts should be a lesson in appreciation.

Having decided what they will do, the children can begin the project and can select the colors that most nearly satisfy the ideas they have in mind, starting with the central figure or object and working toward the edges. The mosaics can be more exciting if they are pasted on a background of colored paper or cardboard. Interesting variations can also be made from sample books of wall-paper, which are a generally available source of colored papers. As the styles and patterns change, these sample books are discarded by the wallpaper stores.

Children can make slightly more complex mosaics by combining a variety of materials. If they can find interesting gravel and pebbles, or varieties of seeds, pods, or types of grains, they can make interesting mosaics by assembling these in various combinations. For mosaics with weight, like those using seeds or pebbles, it is necessary to use a type of glue that has greater strength than ordinary library paste used for paper work. There are a number of excellent milk-white liquid glues on the market that are easy to use and exceedingly strong.

To make a mosaic with tiles is slightly more complex, but not too difficult to try in the upper elementary grades. If a kiln is available, children can easily make their own tiles by rolling out clay with a rolling pin and coating it with a one-fire glaze or an engobe. When it is stiff enough, cut it into small rectangles one-half inch square or smaller. These can be fired and are thereafter ready to apply to a board. If no kiln is available, large quantities of scrap tile can be obtained from tile setters. At the end of each day, tile setters throw away a large box of scrap tile,

---

Figure 10-2. Challenging crafts experiences often grow out of the use of everyday materials. The excellent methods of modern packaging offer almost unlimited opportunity for challenging the ingenuity of children in the crafts program. (Reproduced courtesy of the Bureau of Publications, Baltimore Public Schools)

Figure 10-3. In the early Pompeian paintings and the late Hellenistic mosaics, there are many scenes from everyday life and many still lifes. This Roman mosaic of glass cubes dates from the first century B.C. and shows a great interest in the precise observation of nature. The artist has developed a fine composition with a strong feeling for space. The excellent treatment of light and dark colors sets the main figures apart from the background, while retaining a very subtle use of shading. (Reproduced courtesy of The Metropolitan Museum of Art, New York. Gift of J. Pierpont Morgan, 1917)

10-2

10-3

the pieces remaining from corners and edges they have had to cut. Several days' collection of these would provide an adequate supply with which to begin a ceramic tile mosaic. The scraps can be broken up with a hammer, but it is best to use a pair of tile nippers, which are available at any hardware store. The trick to cutting tiles with nippers is to catch only the very edge of the tile and then snap it. Children can quickly master this method of cutting tiles.

When a sufficient number of small pieces are broken and a design planned and marked off on a piece of plywood or masonite, the tile setting begins. It is first necessary to build a small wooden wall all around the edge of the plywood to hold in place the cement that will eventually go between the pieces of tile. For the moment, the children simply glue the tiles to the plywood with white liquid glue. When the design is complete and firmly set, the children pour a thin mixture of cement, sand, and water, called *grout*, over the entire mosaic, filling the spaces between the tiles. After the grout has been worked down into these spaces, dry concrete is dusted over the surface and rubbed with a cloth. This dry concrete aids in the rapid setting of the grout and cleans the mosaic at the same time. When this is done, the children place damp cloths or wet paper towels over the mosaic and allow them to remain for a day or two to prevent cracks from forming in the grout area. Then the mosaic can be scrubbed clean with a scrubbing brush and soap, and it is a completed project.

BAKED ART

The infinite variety of forms and decoration of breads, cakes, and cookies is amazing. Some bakers have always thought of their products as works of art and have made them not only enjoyably edible but visually enjoyable, as well. As a folk art, baking has primarily been associated with the traditions and customs of the holidays, but like most craftsmen, some bakers have customarily added the element of visual beauty to all their products.

Most school situations cannot afford the opportunity for baking. There are, however, some simple procedures that might be used even under the most limited conditions. The following procedure and recipe are similar to those for salt-ceramic, except that this recipe is for a wheat flour dough. It results in a tough, inedible, but delightful browned cookie. This recipe can be prepared by the children either at school or at home and it can be stored for a day or so if it is kept airtight in Saran wrap.

The child mixes together four cups of flour and one cup of table salt in a large bowl. When these are well mixed, he adds one and one-half cups of water and mixes with a large spoon as thoroughly as possible. Then he kneads this

Figure 10-4. A simple nonedible flour clay dough can be stored in the refrigerator for several weeks if wrapped in air-tight plastic. It is an excellent supplement to clay modeling. Rich effects are attained by over-baking the dough until it is deep brown or by painting the baked pieces.

mixture by hand for about five minutes or until it has an even consistency about like that of modeling clay. After washing and drying his hands, he pulls off a small handful and pats it into a cake about one-half-inch thick on a piece of aluminum foil. Now, what shall it be—a dog, an angel, a boy, an owl, a fish, a horse, Mother? He starts to shape the dough as clay is shaped. It can be cut, pinched, squeezed, modeled, added to, and pressed until the desired shape is obtained. When pieces are joined, the child must take care to see that they are carefully attached either by using a little moisture or by scoring. He can enrich the finished object by creating a variety of textures on parts of the surface by using the points of a fork, buttons, natural objects such as seeds or shells. Some decorative items such as beads, buttons, seeds, and candies can be imbedded into the soft dough before baking. If the object is to hang, a thin wire should be embedded deeply into the soft dough with several inches extending.

The dough, still on the aluminum foil, is now ready for the oven. If the school cafeteria is available, get permission and use it. Otherwise take the objects home or send them home with the children. Often such a project gets parents interested in working together with their children on creative projects. Bake the cookies at 350° for one to two hours, depending on their thickness. They will emerge as strong, golden brown sculptures that are attractive as they are, or they may be painted with acrylic paints or sprayed with a clear acrylic if they are to be preserved indefinitely. For the family that enjoys doing things together, this can be an enjoyable evening activity in which every member of the family can contribute something for the holiday decorations.

Figure 10-5. Hobbyhorse, early-nineteenth century. Children in almost every culture have toys replicating objects of adult living. Today's child wheels about in metal or plastic toy automobiles. A generation earlier, children built toy vehicles from crates and discarded wheels. Still earlier, home-carved hobby horses like the one shown were the joy of small children, who pranced by the hour on spirited steed (The Smithsonian Institution)

Figure 10-6. This hobby horse was made by a young mother using a heavy, cotton man's stocking. Some appliqued spots, a yarn mane, and a heavy dowel stick make it ready for hours of enjoyment and make it a personal "one of a kind" toy with much more personality than a manufactured toy.

Figure 10-7. Rattle, Haida, British Columbia. Wood has always been the preferred medium of the Indians of the Northwest Coast of North America. In addition to their massive wood totem sculptures, they carved ceremonial and utilitarian objects of unusual quality. Among these were the dance rattles in the shape of birds combined with human and animal figures in highly complex compositions. (Museum of the America Indian. Heye Foundation)

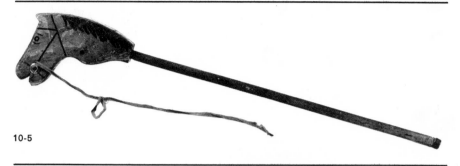

10-5

10-6

10-7

10-8

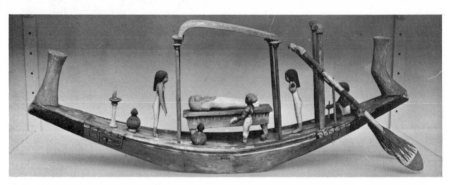

10-9

10-10

TOY MAKING

In recent years, many elementary classrooms have been provided with a small workbench or worktable, a vise, and a small variety of hand tools, such as a saw, hammer, and pliers. Just a hammer and some nails can be sufficient for making very pleasant little wooden toys. To stimulate the imagination, there should always be a scrap box for wooden pieces in the classroom and periodic visits to the school shop or local lumberyard to gather scrap wood. The teacher should try to select interesting shapes of soft wood: pieces of oak or hickory are impossible for the children to nail and can be extremely frustrating to both teacher and child. It takes little motivation for children to begin to build toys, and the variety of shapes in the box will suggest the uses to which the pieces may be put. Older children can use several cans of bright enamel for painting. Younger ones are generally limited to water-based paints, so that if an accident should occur, the paint can easily be washed up. Bottle caps can be nailed to the bottom boards of toys that will be pulled along the floor, to serve as gliders. Again, a scrap box containing buttons, braid, fringe, rickrack, felt scraps, feathers, beads, and old costume jewelry will provide very rich and interesting decoration for the toys. The youngsters can get even more pleasure out of these homemade toys than out of their commercially made metal or plastic ones.

MODEL MAKING

One seldom thinks of model making as an activity of the craftsman, yet model making has been a craft since ancient times. Many fine examples of models remain from the tombs of Egypt, and other examples can be found in many museums from later cultures. The earliest models, human figures, animals, vehicles, and other objects were produced for use in religious or ritual activities and as furnish-

---

Figure 10-8. Model of the City of Burghausen. A common practice among architects is to use models of individual buildings and sometimes of complete cities for planning and for geographical, topographical, and engineering studies. Among the oldest surviving models are those of German cities such as this one of Burghausen. (The Bayerisches Nationalmuseum, Munich)

Figure 10-9. Funerary Boat, Egypt, ca. 2000 B.C. Miniature models have been made since earliest times as ritual or religious objects, votive offerings, incense burners, or tomb furnishings to be buried with the dead for use in afterlife. This model boat, 29″ in length, accurately reproduces the boats used in Egypt 4,000 years ago. (The British Museum, London)

Figure 10-10. Model of a Cattle Stable, Egypt, XI, Dynasty, ca. 2000 B.C. The value and effectiveness of models for educational and historical purpose is evidenced by their wide use in museums and exhibitions where they present graphically the styles, artistic accomplishments, and aesthetic principles of past cultures and distant lands. (The Metropolitan Museum of Art, Museum Excavations, 1919–1920; Rogers Fund supplemented by contribution of Edward S. Harkness)

ings for tombs to be used by the deceased in afterlife. The Haniwa horse (Chapter Two) and the model of weavers (Chapter Nine) are typical examples of models. Today, as they have for centuries, architects produce models along with their plans. No major architectural or city planning project is ever completed without the development and evolution of studies that include both plans and models.

Certain toys, such as puppets, dolls, miniature furniture and household objects, and doll houses, are models, because they reproduce larger objects on a smaller scale. Some models of these toys are so excellent in craftsmanship that they have become works of art and are exhibited in museums.

On many occasions creative model making is a highly desirable school activity. Of course, the children must continue to be inventive, imaginative, and resourceful in their use of materials. Assembling of ready-made models that require little creativity can contribute little or nothing to children's development. Dioramas and peep shows, described earlier, are types of models. When the class studies about other cultures, other countries, new developments in the local community, new developments in exploration and science, new types of housing, and so forth, it has many chances to use model making effectively and to have a goal for student research.

COSTUMES AND DRESS-UP

The desire to dress up and to pretend is shared by most children in the lower elementary grades. There are times when a costume is important in dramatizations, but sometimes just making costumes for the fun of it is in order.

Hats are never a problem. They can be made from paper bags or construction paper. The costumes themselves can be made from large pieces of brown wrapping paper folded double, with an opening cut for the head; the sides are stapled or sewed closed, and the whole is painted or decorated however the child wishes, depending upon the circumstances. Special problems like "let's all make animals" or "let's all be princes or princesses" or "let's make party clothes" can serve as

Figure 10-11. Cloth Ghost Dance Shirt, Sioux Indians. Most of the Sioux's art was concentrated on items carried on the person or worn. The designs, taken from dreams or visions have the naive charm of children's drawings. This shirt, used in the ghost dance, was part of a mystical-religious movement at the end of the 19th century which hoped to get the aid of dead ancestors in freeing the Indian of the white oppressors. (Museum of the American Indian, Heye Foundation)

Figure 10-12. Dress-up is one of the child's earliest, most spontaneous games. It is easy to utilize this interest in costuming as part of the activities of the art class, for plays, parades, and pageants are always fun. (Photograph by Ed Leos)

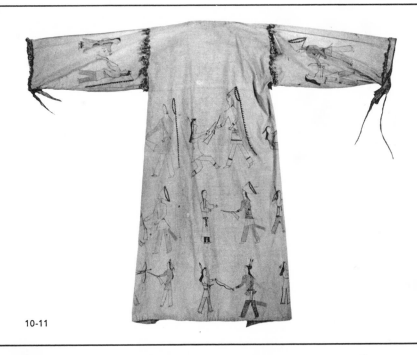

10-11

10-12

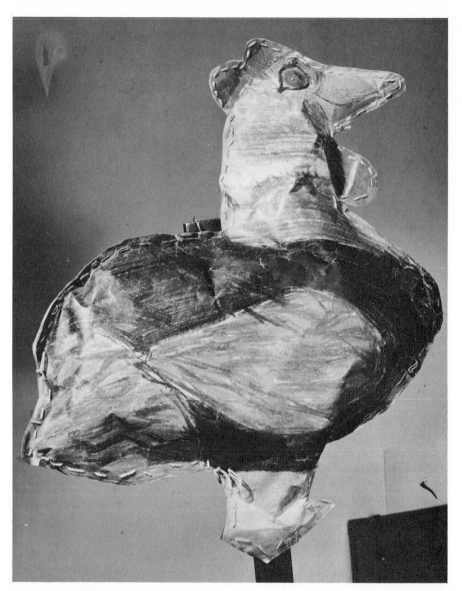

Figure 10-13. This oversized chicken is made from wrapping paper stuffed with crumpled news-paper and then stitches around the edges. By inserting a long stick or broom handle in the center before the stitching is complete, it is possible to make these into excellent stick puppets. (Photo-graph by Ed Leos)

challenging motivations. Long paper bags from the drycleaner can be used in the same way as the wrapping paper, only their sides are already closed, and one simply has to open a hole for the head and arms and cut it to a suitable length.

If the project is "cowboys and cowgirls," simple vests, skirts, and neckerchiefs can be made and decorated with fringe or cut paper or painted designs. If it is "spacemen," then perhaps a helmet can be made of a cardboard box, with openings cut for the face and then covered with colored cellophane. Aerials, too, might be added. Discarded clothing will make excellent raw material, and the teacher should allow the children to cut and sew and create their own fashions from these discards.

STUFFED PAPER ANIMALS

Most small children have had stuffed animals to play with during their pre-school and early school years, and they may enjoy making large stuffed animals from brown wrapping paper, yarn, and paint. This can be a challenging project. Each child gets a large, double thickness of brown wrapping paper on which to draw or paint an animal, bird, or fish. The teacher must pay close attention at this stage, so that legs do not become too spindly or tails too thin to be stuffed.

When he has painted a good animal or bird on one of the pieces of paper, the child pins together the two thicknesses and cuts out the profile he has drawn. Then, using wads of crumpled newspapers for stuffing, he can begin to sew around the edge of the figure. When enough of it is closed, more stuffing is gently inserted to inflate the sides. The child continues until he has gone completely around the figure and is back to the starting point. Then the figure is fully stuffed and sewed, and the second side can be painted to match the first or to contrast with it. When all of the figures have been painted, they can be hung around the room as a delightful zoo.

DOLLS

The same procedures used in making puppets can be used to make lovely dolls without strings. Small children can make a very simple doll from a man's stocking. For this they need scissors, a needle and thread, some cotton batting for stuffing, some buttons, ribbon, and perhaps some bits of cloth for clothing. The toe of the stocking will make the arms. It is cut off about 3″ back and then cut in half lengthwise. When folded double, this makes a small, triangular piece, one side of which can be sewed shut and the triangle stuffed. The rest of the foot is split lengthwise several inches up the stocking, and each side of the slit sewed together to form the two legs which are then stuffed with cotton batting. The heel becomes the seat, for this will be a sitting doll. Stuff the heel and enough more of the stocking to make the body, and tie it off with ribbon. Stuff the remainder for a round head, and tie it off. The little bit that remains can become the cap, which turns down over the head. Now the arms can be sewed into place, and with additional ribbons, buttons, and embroidery, a face can be made. A piece of ribbon can make a belt; buttons can be sewed down the front; and cloth can make a shirt or a scarf.

Sometimes these dolls can be sent home with the very youngest children almost finished, and the mother will want to help the child finish or dress the doll. We are anxious for the children to learn to do their own work, but there are definite values inherent in having the mother and child work together.

Other simple dolls can be made with pieces of cotton, wool, or velvet. For a flat doll, the child would draw his pattern on a piece of paper. He would place two pieces of cloth on top of one another, pin them to his pattern, and cut around the pattern lines. He can sew the two pieces of cloth with an overcasting stitch, leaving with the top of the head open for stuffing. If there are features to be added, these can most easily be added before stuffing. Finally, a dress and hat can be made from another piece of material.

IN CONCLUSION

Once an imaginative craft program has been used to enrich the elementary school program, the teacher will need no convincing of its value. Learning becomes easier; work habits improve; children become happier and continually grow in their problem-solving ability. The teacher knows that good materials suited to the age, interests, and needs of the children are essential for an effective program, and that it is necessary to plan carefully in order to carry out interesting and worthwhile projects and activities. It is important that a classroom climate be developed that permits enough freedom for creative thinking and creative work.

On the other hand, the teacher must exert sufficient control and provide enough direction and motivation to teach good work habits. Craft work must be creative, calling upon the child to use his initiative, resourcefulness, and imagination in solving the problems presented. All crafts should provide sufficient problems so to challenge each child so that he can grow. All crafts should foster the aesthetic growth of the child and make him more aware of the beauty in the world about him. All crafts should permit the child to learn about materials, to gain respect for their limitations, and yet to explore fully their possibilities. Crafts are satisfying, crafts bring pleasure. There is no better feeling than the one that accompanies creative production and the delight of a job well done.

10-14	10-15	10-16

Figure 10-14. The unique toy sculpture of William Accorsi shows how the most commonplace discard can be revitalized when put to a new use. By assembling scraps of wood and an amazing variety of old objects, the artist has created a whole new world of delightful sculpture. (The Museum of Contemporary Crafts of the American Craftsmen's Council)

Figure 10-15. Cornhusk doll from Southeastern United States. There is a large group of art in America which comes from those who have not had special study in art techniques. It exemplifies the talent and art spirit of the people. (Southern Highlands Craftsmen's Guild, Photograph by Edward L. Du Puy)

Figure 10-16. Doll by Irena Martens. Combining cloth, feathers, papier-mâché, and miscellaneous materials this artist has made an unusual, humorous figure quite unlike anything tradition would dictate. There is no "right" in crafts: there is no perfection. There are only learning and development —and time honored differences of taste and temperament. And there is, above all, meaning in crafts. (Museum of Contemporary Crafts of the American Craftsmen's Council)

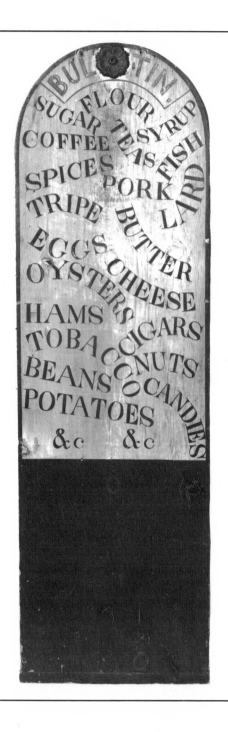

bibliography

ART EDUCATION THEORY AND PRACTICE

Bannon, Laura. *Mind Your Child's Art*. New York: Pelligrini and Cudahy, 1952.

Barkan, Manuel, *Through Art to Creativity*. Boston: Allyn and Bacon, Inc., 1960.

Bland, Jane C., *Art of the Young Child*. New York: The Museum of Modern Art, 1958.

Cole, Natalie Robinson. *Children's Art From Deep Down Inside*. New York: The John Day Company, Inc., 1966.

————, *The Arts in the Classroom*. New York: John Day Co., Inc., 1940.

Conant, Howard, and Arne Randall, *Art in Education*. Peoria, Ill.: Charles A. Bennett Co., Inc., 1959.

Conrad, George, *The Process of Art Education in the Elementary School*. Englewood Cliffs, N. J.: Prentice-Hall, Inc., 1964.

D'Amico, Victor, *Creative Teaching in Art*. Scranton, Pa.: International Textbook Company, 1955.

de Francesco, Italo L., *Art Education: Its Means and Ends.* New York: Harper & Row, Publishers, 1958.

Erdt, Margaret H., *Teaching Art in the Elementary School*, rev. ed. New York: Holt, Rinehart & Winston, Inc., 1962.

Feldman, Edmund B, *Becoming Human Through Art*. Englewood Cliffs, N. J.: Prentice-Hall, Inc., 1970.

Gaitskell, Charles, and Hurwitz, Al, *Children and Their Art*. New York: Harcourt, Brace & World, Inc., 1970.

Gezari, Temima, *Footprints and New Worlds*. New York: Reconstructionist Press, 1957.

Hoover, F. Louis, *Art Activities for the Very Young.* Worcester, Mass.: The Davis Publications, Inc., 1961.

Horn, George F., *Art For Today's Schools.* Worcester, Mass.: Davis Publications, Inc., 1967.

Jameson, Kenneth, *Art and the Young Child*. New York: The Viking Press, 1968.

Jefferson, Blanche, *Teaching Art to Children*. Boston: Allyn and Bacon, Inc., 2nd edition, 1963.

Kaufman, Irving. *Art and Education in Contemporary Culture*. New York: The Macmillan Company, 1966.

Keiler, Manfred L., *Art in the Schoolroom*. Lincoln, Neb.: University of Nebraska Press, 1955.

————, *The Art in Teaching Art*. Lincoln, Neb.: University of Nebraska Press, 1961.

Kellogg, Rhoda and Scott O'Dell. *The Psychology of Children's Art*. New York: CRM— Random House, Inc., 1967.

This nineteenth-century store sign from Vermont uses words in a way that is both eye-catching and aesthetically pleasing (The Smithsonian Institution).

Knudson, Estelle, and Ethel M. Christensen, *Children's Art Education*. Peoria, Ill.: Charles A. Bennett Co., Inc., 1957.

Lansing, Kenneth, *Art, Artists, and Art Education*. New York: McGraw-Hill Book Company, 1969.

Lark-Horovitz, B., and Hilda Lewis, March Luca, *Understanding Children's Art for Better Teaching*. Columbus: Charles Merrill Publishing Company, 1967.

Hilda Lewis, ed. *Child Art: The Beginning of Self Affirmation*. San Francisco: Diablo Press, 1966.

Linderman, Earl, and Donald Herberholtz, *Developing Artistic and Perceptual Awareness*. Dubuque, Iowa: Wm. C. Brown Co., 2nd. edition, 1969.

Lindstrom, Miriam, *Children's Art*. Berkeley: University of California Press, 1960.

Lowenfeld, Viktor, *Your Child and His Art*. New York: The Macmillan Company, 1954.

———, and Lambert Brittain, *Creative and Mental Growth*, rev. ed. New York: The Macmillan Company, 1970.

McFee, June K., *Preparation for Art*. Belmont, Calif.: Wadsworth Publishing Company, Inc., 1961, 1970.

McIlvain, Dorothy S., *Art for the Primary Grades*. New York: G. P. Putnam's Sons, 1961.

McLeish, Minnie, *Beginnings: Teaching Art to Children*, rev. ed. New York: Studio Publications, 1953.

Mendelowitz, Daniel M., *Children Are Artists*. Stanford, Calif.: Stanford University Press, 1953.

Merritt, Helen. *Guiding Free Expression in Children's Art*. New York: Holt, Rinehart & Winston, 1964.

Mitchell, John B., *Teaching Art to Children*. Boston: Allyn and Bacon, Inc., 1959.

Packwood, Mary M., ed. *Art Education in the Elementary School*. National Art Education Association, 1967.

Robertson, Seonaid, *Rosegarden and Labyrinth: A Study In Art Education*. New York: Barnes and Noble, 1963.

Rueschoff, Phil H., and Evelyn Swartz, *Teaching Art in the Elementary School*. New York: The Ronald Press Co., 1969.

Schultz, Harold A., and J. Harlan Shores, *Art in the Elementary School*. Urbana: University of Illinois Press, 1948.

Smith, James A., *Setting Conditions for Creative Teaching*. Boston: Allyn and Bacon, Inc., 1966.

Viola, Wilhelm, *Child Art*. London: University of London Press, 1952.

Wachowiak, F. and R. K. Ramsey. *Emphasis: Art*. Scranton, Pa.: International Textbook Co., 1965.

Wickiser, Ralph L., *An Introduction to Art Education*. New York: Harcourt, Brace & World, Inc., 1957.

CRAFTS IN EDUCATION

Brown, Mamie E., *Elementary Handcrafts for Elementary Schools*. New York: Exposition Press, 1956.

Elsworth, Maude, and Michael Andrews, *Growing with Art*. Chicago: Benj. H. Sanborn Co., 1950.

Fearing, Kelly, and Evelyn Beard, *Our Expanding Vision*. Austin, Texas: W. S. Benson and Company, 1960.

Grimm, Gretchen, and Catherine Skeets, *Crafts Adventures for Children*. Milwaukee: Bruce Publishing Co., 1952.

Hils, Karl, *Crafts for All*. Newton Centre, Mass.: Charles T. Branford Co., 1960.

Ickis, Marguerite, *Arts and Crafts*. New York: A. S. Barnes & Co., Inc., 1943.

Mosley, Spencer, Pauline Johnson, and Hazel Koening, *Crafts Design*. Belmont, Calif.: Wadsworth Publishing Company, Inc., 1962.

Reed, Carl, and Joseph Orze, *Art from Scrap*. Worcester, Mass.: The Davis Publications, Inc., 1960.

Robertson, Seonaid, *Creative Crafts in Education*. Cambridge, Mass.: Robert Bentley, Inc., 1953.

Slivka, Rose, Aileen Webb and Margaret Patch, *The Crafts of the Modern World*. New York: The Horizon Press, 1968.

Wankelman, Willard, Philip Wigg, and Marietta Wigg, *A Handbook of Arts and Crafts for Elementary and Junior High School Teachers*. Dubuque, Iowa: Wm. C. Brown Co., 1961.

Zechlin, Ruth, *Complete Book of Handcrafts*. Newton Centre, Mass.: Charles T. Branford Co., 1959.

CRAFTS PROCESSES

Accorsi, William, *Toy Sculpture*. New York: Reinhold Publishing Corp., 1965.

Ahlberg, Gudrun, and O. Jarneryd, *Block and Silk Screen Printing*. New York: Sterling Publishing Co., Inc., 1961.

Alexander, Marthann, *Fifteen Simple Ways to Weave*. Bloomington, Ill.: McKnight & McKnight, Pubs., 1954.

———, *Simple Weaving*. New York: Taplinger Publishing Company, Inc., 1969.

Allard, Mary, *Rug Making Technique and Design*. Philadelphia: Chilton Co., Book Division, 1963.

Aller, Doris, *Wood Carving Book*. Menlo Park, Calif.: Lane Book Company, 1951.

———, *Handmade Rugs*. Menlo Park, Calif.: Lane Book Company, 1953.

———, and Diana Lee Aller, *Sunset Mosaics*. Menlo Park, Calif.: Lane Book Company, 1959.

Andrews, Michael, *Creative Printmaking*. Englewood Cliffs, N. J.: Prentice-Hall, Inc., 1963.

———, *Sculpture and Ideas*. Englewood Cliffs, N. J.: Prentice-Hall, Inc., 1965.

Angrane, Bruce, *Sculpture in Paper*. New York: Thomas Y. Crowell Company, 1957.

Argiro, Larry, *Mosaic Art Today*. Scranton, Pa.: International Textbook Company, 1961.

Arnold, James, *The Shell Book of Country Crafts*. New York: Hastings House Publishers, 1969.

Atwater, Mary Meigs, *Byways in Hand-Weaving*. New York: The Macmillan Company, 1954.

Baird, Bill, *The Art of the Puppet.* New York: The Macmillan Company, 1966.

Ball, Carlton and Janice Lovous, *Making Pottery without a Wheel: Texture and Form in Clay.* New York: Reinhold Publishing Corp., 1965.

Baranski, Matthew, *Mask Making.* Worcester, Mass.: The Davis Publications, Inc., 1954.

Barford, George, *Clay in the Classroom.* Worcester, Mass.: The Davis Publications, Inc., 1964.

Batchelder, Marjorie, *The Puppet Theatre Handbook.* New York: Harper & Row, Publishers, 1947.

Beard, Geoffrey, *Modern Ceramics.* New York: Studio Vista/E. P. Dutton and Co., Inc., 1969.

Becher, Lotte, *Handweaving.* New York: Thomas Y. Crowell Company, 1954.

Betts, Victoria, *Exploring Papier-Mâché.* Worcester, Mass.: The Davis Publications, Inc., 1955.

Birrell, Verla, The *Textile Arts.* New York: Harper & Row, Publishers, 1959.

Blumenau, Lili, *The Art and Crafts of Handweaving.* New York: Crown Publishers, Inc., 1955.

Bodor, John J. *Rubbing and Textures.* New York: Reinhold Publishing Corp., 1965.

Brommer, Gerald F., *Wire Sculpture and other Three Dimensional Construction.* Worcester, Mass.: Davis Publications, Inc., 1966.

Brownley Albert, *How to Paint and Stencil Textiles*, 4th ed. Brooklyn: Alby Studio, 1952.

Bufano, Remo, *Book of Puppetry.* New York: The Macmillan Company, 1950.

Carter, Jean, *Creative Play with Fabrics and Thread.* New York: Taplinger Publishing Company, Inc., 1969.

Cataldo, John W., *Words & Calligraphy for Children.* New York: Reinhold Book Corp., 1969.

Christopher, Frederick J., and Lili Blumenau, *Hand Loom Weaving.* New York: Dover Publications, Inc., 1954.

Cizek, Franz, *Children's Colored Paper Work.* New York: Stechert-Hafner Service Agency, Inc., 1927.

Conran, Terence, *Printed Textile Design.* New York: Studio Publications, 1957.

Cox, Doris, and Barbara Warren, *Creative Hands.* New York: John Wiley & Sons, Inc., 1951.

Duncan, Julia Hamlin, and Victor D'Amico, *How to Make Pottery and Ceramic Sculpture.* New York: Museum of Modern Art. Distributed by Simon and Schuster, Inc., 1947.

Eliscu, Frank, *Sculpture Techniques in Clay, Wax, Slate.* Great Neck, N. Y.: Arts and Crafts Book Club, 1961.

Enthoven, Jacqueline. *Stitchery for Children: A Manual for Teachers, Parents, and Children.* New York: Reinhold Publishing Corp, 1964.

Erikson, Janet Dobbs, *Block Printing on Textiles.* New York: Watson-Guptill Publications, Inc., 1961.

Gorbaty, Norman, *Printmaking with a Spoon.* New York: Reinhold Publishing Corp., 1960.

Greenberg, Pearl. *Children's Experiences in Art: Drawing and Painting.* New York: Reinhold Publishing Corp., 1966.

Guild, Vera P., *Creative Use of Stitches.* Worcester, Mass.: The Davis Publications, Inc., 1964.

Hartung, Rolf, *Creative Textile Design: Thread and Fabric.* New York: Reinhold Publishing Corp., 1963.

————, *More Creative Textile Design: Color and Texture.* New York: Reinhold Publishing Corp., 1964.

Heller, Jules, *Printmaking Today*. New York: Holt, Rinehart & Winston, Inc., 1958.

Hendrickson, Edwin, *Mosaics: Hobby and Art*. New York: Hill & Wang, Inc., 1957.

Herberholz, Donald and Barbara. *A Child's Pursuit of Art: 110 Motivations for Drawing, Painting, and Modeling*. Dubuque, Iowa: Wm. C. Brown Company Publishers.

Hobson, A. F., *Paper Sculpture*. Leicester, England: Dryad, Ltd., 1956.

Home, Ruth M., *Ceramics for the Potter*. Peoria, Ill.: Charles A. Bennett Co., Inc., 1953.

Horn, George F., *The Crayon*. Worcester, Mass.: Davis Publications, Inc., 1968.

———, *Posters: Designing, Making, Reproducing*. Worcester, Mass.: The Davis Publications, Inc., 1964.

Jefferson, Blanche, Barbara Fredette, Barbara McGeary, Clyde McGeary, *My World of Art Series*. Boston: Allyn and Bacon, Inc., 1963–1964.

Jenkins, Louisa, and Barbara Mills. *The Art of Making Mosaics*. Princeton, N.J.: Van Nostrand Reinhold Company, 1957.

Johnson, Ilse and Nika Standen Hazelton, *Cookies and Breads: The Baker's Art*. New York: The Reinhold Publishing Corp., 1967.

Johnson, Lillian, *Papier-Mâché*. New York: David McKay Co., Inc., 1958.

Johnston, Mary Grace, *Paper Sculpture*. Worcester, Mass.: The Davis Publications, Inc., 1952.

Johnston, Pauline, *Creating with Paper*. Seattle: University of Washington Press, 1958.

Kafka, Frances J., *Linoleum Block Printing*. Bloomington, Ill.: McKnight & McKnight, Pubs., 1955.

Karasz, Mariska, *Adventures in Stitches and More Adventures, Fewer Stitches*. New York: Funk & Wagnalls Co., 1959.

Kenny, John B., and Carla. *The Art of Papier-Mâché*. Philadelphia: Chilton Book Co., 1969.

Krevitsky, Nik. *Stitchery: Art and Craft*. New York: Reinhold Publishing Corp., 1966.

Krum, Josephine R., *Hand-Built Pottery*. Scranton, Pa.: International Textbook Company, 1960.

Laliberte, Norman, and Alex Mogelon, *Painting With Crayons: History and Modern Techniques*. New York: Reinhold Publishing Corp., 1967.

——— and Sterling McIlhany. *Banners and Hangings: Design and Construction*. New York: Reinhold Publishing Corp., 1966.

——— and Alex Mogelon. *Silhouettes, Shadows, and Cutouts*. New York: Reinhold, 1968.

Lanchester, Waldo, *Hand Puppets and String Puppets*. Peoria, Ill.: Charles A. Bennett Co., Inc., 1953.

Leeming, Joseph, *Fun with Fabrics*. Philadelphia: J. B. Lippincott Co., 1950.

Linderman, Earl W. *Invitation to Vision: Ideas and Imaginations for Art*. Dubuque, Iowa: Wm. C. Brown Company Publishers, 1967.

Lipski, Tadeusz, *Paper Sculpture*. New York: Thomas Y. Crowell Company, 1948.

Lord, Lois, *Collage and Construction in Elementary and Junior High Schools*. Worcester, Mass.: The Davis Publications, Inc., 1958.

Lynch, John, *Mobile Design*. New York: Thomas Y. Crowell Company, 1955.

Merton, George, *The Hand Puppets*. New York: Thomas Nelson & Sons, 1957.

———, *Marionette*. New York: Thomas Nelson & Sons, 1957.

Moran, Jean Mary. *Art: of Wonder & a World*. New York: Art Education, Inc., Publishers, 1967.

Nelson, Glenn C., *Ceramics*. New York: Holt, Rinehart & Winston, Inc., 1960.

Petterson, Henry and Ray Gerring, *Exploring With Paint*. New York: Reinhold Publishing Corp., 1964.

Rainey, Sarita. *Weaving Without A Loom*. Worcester, Mass,; Davis Publications, Inc., 1966.

Randall, Arne W., *Murals for Schools*. Worcester, Mass.: The Davis Publications, Inc., 1960.

Rasmusen, Henry N. *Printmaking with Monotype*. Philadelphia: Chilton Book Company, Book Division, 1960.

Rhodes, Daniel, *Clay and Glazes for the Potter*. Philadelphia: Chilton Book Company, Book Division, 1957.

Rosenberg, *Children Make Murals and Sculpture: Experience in Community Art Projects*. New York: Reinhold Publishing Corp., 1962.

Röttger, Ernst and Deiter Klante, *Creative Drawing: Point and Line*. New York: Reinhold Publishing Corp., 1964.

Röttger, Ernst, *Creative Clay Design*. New York: Reinhold Publishing Corp., 1962.

———, *Creative Paper Design*. New York: Reinhold Publishing Corp., 1961.

———, *Creative Wood Design*. New York: Reinhold Publishing Corp., 1961.

Simpson, Lillian E. and Marjorie Weir, *The Weaver's Craft*. Peoria, Ill.: Charles A. Bennett Co., Inc., 1957.

Sister Magdalen Mary, I. H. M., *Mosaics for Everyone*. Los Angeles: Immaculate Heart College, 1958.

Struppeck, Jules, *The Creation of Sculpture*. New York: Holt, Rinehart & Winston, Inc., 1952.

Supensky, Thomas G., *Ceramic Art in the School Program*. Worcester, Mass.: Davis Publications, Inc., 1967.

Timmons, Virginia Gayheart. *Painting in the School Program*. Worcester, Mass.: The Davis Publications, Inc., 1968.

Van Dommelen, David B. *Decorative Wall Hangings: Art with Fabric*. New York: Funk & Wagnalls, 1962.

Villard, Paul, *A First Book of Ceramics*. New York: Funk & Wagnalls, 1969.

Weiss, Harvey, *Clay, Wood and Wire*. New York: William R. Scott, Inc., 1956.

———, *Paper, Ink and Roller*. New York: William R. Scott, Inc., 1958.

Wildenhain, Marguerite, *Pottery: Form and Expression*. New York: Reinhold Publishing Corp., 1962.

Williams, Guy R. *Making Mobiles*. New York: Emerson Books, Inc., 1969.

Woods, Gerald, *Introducing Woodcuts*. New York: Watson-Guptill Publications, 1969.

Young, Joseph L., *Course in Making Mosaics*. New York: Reinhold Publishing Corp., 1957.

Zarbock, Barbara J., *The Complete Book of Rug Hooking*. New York: Van Nostrand Company, 1969.

ART AND CRAFTS HISTORY AND APPRECIATION

Alexander, Eugenie, *Art for Young People*. London: Mills & Boon, Ltd., 1958.

Beaumont, Cyril W., *Puppets and Puppetry*. New York: Studio Publications, 1958.

Bossert, Helmuth T., *Folk Art of Europe*. New York: Frederick A. Praeger, Inc., 1953.

————, *Folk Art of Primitive People*. New York: Frederick A. Praeger, Inc., 1955.

Chandler, Anna C., *Story Lives of Master Artists*. Philadephia: J. B. Lippincott Co., 1953.

Christensen, Erwin O., *Index of American Design*. New York: The Macmillan Company, 1950.

Davis, Beverly Jeanne, *Chant of the Centuries*. Austin, Texas: W. S. Benson and Co., 1969.

Dockstater, Frederick I., *Indian Art in America*. Greenwich, Conn.: N. Y. Graphic Society, 1961.

Dörner, Gerd, *Folk Art of Mexico*. New York: Barnes & Noble, Inc., 1963.

Douglas, Frederick Huntington, and René D'Harnocourt, *Indian Art of the United States*. New York: Museum of Modern Art, 1941.

Eaton, Allen Hendershott, *Handicrafts of New England*. New York: Harper & Row, Publishers, 1949.

Elsen, Albert E., *Purposes of Art*. New York: Holt, Rinehart & Winston, Inc., 1962.

Faulkner, Raymond, Edwin Ziegfeld, and Gerald Hill, *Art Today*, rev. ed. New York: Holt, Rinehart & Winston, Inc., 1966.

Feldman, Edmund B. *Art as Image and Idea*. Englewood Cliffs, N. J.: Prentice-Hall, Inc., 1967.

Fleming, William, *Arts and Ideas*. New York: Holt, Rinehart & Winston, Inc., 1963.

Gardner, Helen, *Art Through the Ages*, rev. ed. New York: Harcourt, Brace & World, Inc., 1959.

Gombrich, Ernest, *The Story of Art*. Greenwich, Conn.: N. Y. Graphic Society, 1954.

Hastie, Reid and Christian Schmidt, *Encounter With Art*. New York: McGraw-Hill Book Company, 1969.

Hillyer, Virgil M., and Edward G. Huey, *Child's History of Art*. New York: Appleton-Century-Crofts, 1951.

Hunt, Kari, and Bernice W. Carlson, *Masks and Mark Makers*. Nashville: Abingdon Press, 1961.

Janson, Horst W., *History of Art*. Englewood Cliffs, N. J.: Prentice-Hall, Inc., 1962.

————, *Story of Painting for Young People*. New York: Harry N. Abrams, Inc., 1952.

Kessler, Leonard, *Art Is Everywhere*. New York: Dodd, Mead & Co., 1958.

Lichten, Francis, *Folk Art of Rural Pennsylvania*. New York: Charles Scribner's Sons, 1946.

Lipman, Jean Herzberg, *American Folk Art in Wood, Metal and Stone*. New York: Pantheon Books, Inc., 1948.

Lowry, Bates. *The Visual Experience: An Introduction to Art*. Englewood Cliffs, N. J.: Prentice-Hall, Inc., 1967.

Manley, Seon, *Adventures in Making: The Romance of Crafts Around the World*. New York: Vanguard Press, 1959.

Meyers, Bernard, *Understanding the Arts*, rev. ed. New York: Holt, Rinehart & Winston, Inc., 1958.

Myers, Bernard S. *Art and Civilization*. New York: McGraw-Hill Book Company, 1967.

Nicholas, Florence W., Carl J. Heyne, Jr., Margaret M. Lee, and Mabel B. Trilling, *Art for Young America*. Peoria, Ill.: Charles A. Bennett Co., Inc., 1960.

Munsterberg, Hugo, *The Folk Arts of Japan*. Rutland, Vt.: Charles E. Tuttle Co., 1958.

Riley, Olive, *Masks and Magic*. New York: Studio Publications, 1955.

———, *Your Art Heritage*. New York: McGraw-Hill Book Company, 1952.

Runes, Dagobert D., and H. G. Schrickel, *Encyclopedia of the Arts*. New York: Philosophical Library, Inc., 1945.

Schinneller, James A., *Art: Search and Self-Discovery*. Scranton, Pa.: International Textbook Company, 1968, 1969.

Taylor, Joshua C. *Learning To Look: A Handbook for the Visual Arts*. Chicago: University of Chicago Press, 1957.

Weibel, Adele C., *Two Thousand Years of Textiles*. New York: Pantheon Books, Inc., 1952.

DESIGN

Adams, Edward, David Van Dommelen, and George Pappas, *Design at Work: Its Forms and Functions*. University Park: The Pennsylvania State University Press, 1960.

Albers, Anni, *On Designing*. Harford: Wesleyan University Press, 1959.

Beitler, Ethel Jane, and B. C. Lockhart, *Design for You*. New York: John Wiley & Sons, Inc., 1961.

Collier, Graham, *Form, Space, and Vision: Discovering Design Through Drawing*. Englewood Cliffs, N. J.: Prentice-Hall, Inc., 1967.

Emerson, Sybil, *Design: A Creative Approach*. Scranton, Pa.: International Textbook Company, 1957.

Mulvey, Frank, *Graphic Perception of Space*. New York: Van Nostrand Reinhold Company, 1969.

INDEX